Dear Marje...

Marjorie Proops

Dear Marje...

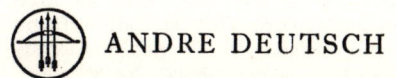 ANDRE DEUTSCH

First published 1976 by
André Deutsch Limited
105 Great Russell Street London WC1

Printed in Great Britain by
Ebenezer Baylis and Son Ltd, The Trinity Press
Worcester, and London

ISBN 0 233 96791 5

Author's Note

The identity of people who write to me seeking advice is never revealed. For this reason,
the letters in this book are based on samples
of letters sent to me; they have all been
edited and rewritten. They are not verbatim
copies and details which might identify
individuals have been changed. Nevertheless,
the situations and circumstances are factually
based on real human dilemmas.

Grateful thanks are due to the *Daily
Mirror* for permission to reproduce copy-
right material, and to Sue Tranter, whose
help and research have been invaluable.

Contents

Introduction

To drop a name, Dr Ramsey, who was at the time Archbishop of Canterbury, once said to me, 'Where has the Church appeared to have failed people that they need to seek help from you?' I was not so big-headed as to assume he meant me personally. He was musing about the reasons why troubled citizens who might be expected to look for help from men of the cloth search for it instead from the advice columnists.

In the twenty years or so since I started handing out advice in newspaper and magazine columns, I estimate that close to a million people have written to me. Add to that immense number those who have written to the other half dozen or so columnists doing similar work and you are bound to reach the sobering conclusion that we fill (or endeavour to fill) a vast need which neither the religious bodies, nor the social services, the doctors or psychiatrists, the welfare workers or the voluntary help organisations can, it seems, adequately answer.

I have noted a certain amount of resentment on the part of some specialist professionals who either believe we're taking the bread out of their mouths, or cast doubts upon our expertise to deal with the kind of problems which spill on our desks in such formidable numbers. One such professional – a lawyer – sneeringly referred to me as Queen of the Agony Aunties and asked me what right I thought I had to set myself up as an oracle. He was less kind than the avuncular Archbishop who was convinced that advice columnists perform an essential and invaluable function, or than the many psychiatrists, psycho-therapists and doctors who have expressed similar views.

I *know* how useful we are. For the fact is that very few of the thousands and thousands of people who write to us would seek help at all if we didn't exist. Many people with personal problems are afraid to face doctors, scared of anyone who might seem to be authoritarian. They fear the pointing moralising finger of blame. Or they are too inarticulate to express themselves verbally.

It's something, I think, to do with the attitude of many GPs towards their patients' personal problems. Doctors with huge NH lists and little time for comforting platitudes – let alone considered and helpful advice – often say, 'Now pull yourself together, Mrs Smith', and write out a prescription for tranquillisers. In any case, only comparatively few doctors know enough about sexual difficulties to be able to offer much help in this particular area of need, even if they had the time to try to solve such problems.

It always seems astonishing to me that I am frequently invited by professors at teaching hospitals to give lectures and talks to medical students about the kind of problems they will one day be faced with in their practices – I, who have no degrees and few special qualifications other than long experience and self-education (with a little help from my professional friends).

'How did it all begin?' is a question I am often asked. It began accidentally, when I was Woman's Editor of the now defunct *Daily Herald*.

Among the contributors whose columns I put regularly into my women's pages was a brilliant and dedicated young woman whose pen name was Mary Marshall. She occupied a small room near my office and produced her letters and answers copy for the paper and wrote personal letters to all her readers, helping them to sort out their difficulties. One day she failed to arrive for work. She'd been rushed into hospital. Three days later, she was dead. And I soon realised what a gap she'd left – not only as a wise and good journalist, and a friend – but as an adviser to so many people who relied on her.

I tried to find someone to take over her column but it was a hopeless task. It had to be a member of the National Union of Journalists for the *Herald* was a union closed shop. It had to be a journalist who could do this specialised work and they are not thick on the ground even now. In those days, more than twenty years ago, they were very scarce indeed.

As time went by, the mound of letters on the desk in the room next door grew, until one evening I decided I'd better take them home and try to answer some of them, at least. I spent half the night reading. And worrying. Many of the problems seemed to me to be insuperable. They were complicated and often heartbreaking and I was desperate. Next day I rang a psychologist, an old friend named Dr Eustace Chesser who had a practice in Harley Street. I cried 'Help, help,' and told him about the letters. He said, 'Bring some round to my rooms lunchtime. I'll give you a bowl of soup and we'll see what we can do.'

That was the start of my first crash course in How To Be An Advice Columnist.

Every lunch hour he could spare I was there in Harley Street with my notebook and the letters. He didn't attempt to answer them. He taught me how to analyse them, even to analysing handwriting. He taught me how to find the nub of a problem which might be buried in a mass of irrelevancies. A problem apparently, at first sight, about a mother-in-law, he explained, could indicate a sexual hang-up when you delved between the lines.

He lectured me about the traditional psychological syndromes: father-son conflicts, mother-daughter conflicts, frigidity, impotence and so on. He gave me books to read and I abandoned the escapist whodunits I usually took to bed and took, instead, sex manuals and heavy works by psychologists and psychiatrists and other specialists. He also advised me to study Marriage Guidance and I did another crash course.

Meanwhile, I began to answer readers' letters, timidly and filled with doubts about my capability. But Dr Chesser was always available for consultation, ever patient, sensible and practical, and gradually I became more confident. A few people wrote back and said the advice worked or things seemed a lot easier or they felt much happier. Even if they only wrote, 'I feel better now I've got it all off my chest,' I felt there was, at any rate, a cathartic value in the work I was now finding so fascinating and rewarding.

I *

I started up the Mary Marshall column in the paper again, doing it myself and it seemed to be going well. I continued to do my homework and Eustace Chesser regularly quizzed me on my lessons and redirected me when necessary. I became deeply interested in everything to do with social as well as sexual problems.

Most people believe that advice columnists deal only with sex. You get a lot of the nudge-nudge treatment in this job. Sometimes, at dinner parties, sitting next to elderly, salacious gentlemen, you get a nudge in the ribs and the chortling citizen will say, 'I bet you get a lot of juicy ones, eh?' Others think the whole thing's a real scream.

'You must laugh your head off' they say, 'at some of the letters you get.'

I wish I could invite them to read just one day's distressing mail. They'd soon stop thinking of the job in terms of a sexy nudge or a scream of mirth.

Although the Mary Marshall column in the *Herald* was satisfying to me – and, it appeared, useful to the readers – I was beginning to be restless. Percy Cudlipp, the editor, had left and I felt bereft by his departure. He'd been very good to me and for me, encouraging me and giving me the confidence I lacked. For I needed constant reassurance, not only in this specialised field of journalism I'd taken on, but in every aspect of my work. He gave it to me, courteously and humorously.

The *Herald* was very much a male-orientated organisation, like most newspapers, and Women's Lib hadn't been invented. As the only executive woman, I had my problems but Percy Cudlipp's sensitivity – he was a gentlemanly editor, nothing like the rough, tough Hollywood image – made them bearable.

Life was considerably less bearable after he left and when, a few months later, I bumped into his younger brother Hugh at a party, I was ready to take seriously his casual suggestion that I might like to move to the *Daily Mirror*.

Hugh Cudlipp was Editorial Director of the *Mirror* and we'd known each other since the days when I'd started my career as the lowest form of editorial human life – a fashion artist.

*

An insignificant pupil at the several schools I attended (the family moved around a good deal when I was a child, for my publican father was a restless character), the only subject in which I was in any way mildly distinguished was drawing.

I left the last school just before my sixteenth birthday, had three terms at an art school in North East London and got a job in a commercial art studio in the middle of Smithfield meat market.

It wasn't until some years later that I discovered my father had actually paid the boss a premium to get him to take me on his staff.

I was given a rickety table in a corner of the shabby little studio and my small drawing skills were not put to great advantage. The nearest I got to drawing, for some time, was rubbing out the pencil marks on the work of the senior artists. Mostly, I swept floors, kept the place tidy, delivered the artists' work to clients, collected clothes from wholesale manufacturers, and made tea for the staff.

It was, I suppose, useful training. I picked up a ripe vocabulary from the meat porters in the market which came in handy later. And the artists were hell bent on making something out of the plain, bespectacled, scared junior in their midst. Two of them, especially. The head artist was a blonde named May Rose (now in her eighties and still my dearest friend). The number two in seniority was a brilliant sensitive man named Harry Felber.

May Rose wore curious po-shaped hats made of felt in exotic shades of pea green or puce which she kept on in the studio when her hair was showing dark at the roots and one of my jobs was to touch these up every now and then. She'd produce a saucer of peroxide and ammonia and cotton wool and carry on with her drawing while I dabbed away at the partings.

Harry Felber often did sewing jobs in between turning out line sketches of anything from French knickers to beaded evening dresses.

They decided that my plain dull clothes and mousy appearance must be somehow improved.

Harry made me a puce po hat and bought a pair of tweezers

so that my eyebrows could be thinned out. May Rose bought make-up and instructed me on how to use it.

Copying them, I started to smoke – hating it but determined to be sophisticated and glamorous. I painted my colourless plastic glasses frames bright red with May's nail polish and bandied around some of the four-letter words with which the meat porters punctuated every remark.

May and Harry took me to concerts and theatres, to art galleries and exhibitions. They taught me to appreciate colour and design and opened my myopic eyes to a world I never knew existed. I loved them and still do.

But at seventeen, earning fifteen shillings a week, I felt that my career wasn't exactly flourishing and my parents agreed that there wasn't a great future in being a messenger girl. So I set myself up as a freelance fashion artist, trudging around the West End with a portfolio of specimen sketches, trying to get commissions from wholesalers and dress shops.

I met an elderly artist who offered me a desk in his studio off Fleet Street for seven and six a week and gradually I built up a tiny clientèle, selling fashion drawings to mail order catalogues and for ads in magazines.

I hated doing my own commercial travelling, standing miserably watching while hard-faced buyers or art directors thumbed through my portfolio muttering, 'Not bad, might be able to use you some time.'

I earned an average of seven and sixpence per sketch and sometimes only just managed to pay the rent. To make up for the times I couldn't, I swept up and made tea for the elderly artist and was beginning to wonder whether I'd have had a more secure life if I'd become a shorthand typist, when I encountered an artist's agent who offered to include my specimen drawings in his portfolio. The arrangement was that I'd pay him twenty per cent commission on anything he sold. He sold a lot.

I did some fashion drawings for the *Daily Express* and the *Daily Mail*, for the glossy women's magazines and happily (for me, at any rate) had less time for tea making.

One day I had an urgent call from the man I grandly called my agent to rush round pronto to the *Daily Mirror*. 'Come right away,' he said, 'it's urgent.' I said I was a bit inky and paint-splattered but he told me not to stop to tart myself up, just to get moving.

I hurried around to the *Mirror* where he was conferring with the Woman's Editor and a rather wild-looking young man who was pacing about the room shooting fierce glances at me. I was petrified by him, blinking at him through my red-framed specs, hunched into the tweed jacket of the too-big outfit I'd been given in lieu of payment by a hard-up dress manufacturer. Suddenly he stopped pacing, glared at me and invited me to become the resident fashion-artist of the newspaper.

For years and years I retained traces of the original terror I felt when I first met Hugh Cudlipp, then Features Editor of the *Mirror*, subsequently Editorial Director, Chairman of IPC and now Lord Cudlipp. Though I had no reason to fear him, then or ever. He has been, for all these years, one of my kindest friends, responsible for much of the good that has happened to me professionally. He took over, educationally speaking, where May and Harry left off. He made me into 'Dear Marje'.

I've been very lucky in the people I've encountered who have helped, guided and encouraged me to learn new skills, acquire new interests. I owe more to the unnerving Hugh Cudlipp than to anyone who has pushed me another step up the steep and wobbly career ladder.

I don't include the man I married during this early breathless climb, for his influence and help comes within a different category: the category of a husband, rare at the time we married, who recognising my compelling need to work outside the home, supported this need when the social mores of the time demanded that middle-class married girls stayed home and became housewives and mothers. Not career girls, determined to achieve job fulfilment.

Sometimes readers write to me, asking what special qualities a married woman needs to do a demanding job as well as run her home and keep her family happy.

A good, tolerant, patient, intelligent and sensitive husband, I tell them. One who is ready to make sacrifices, share chores, share worries, give support and encouragement and recognise a woman's right to choose a career if she wants to. One who doesn't denigrate her efforts or put her down in order to bolster his own masculine ego. One who doesn't believe that a woman's career is a joke or a bit of self-indulgence or that she works for pin money. One who believes that women have quite as much to contribute to society, to industry, to the professions as have men. One who is, in a word, an adult man, secure enough in his own masculinity never to feel threatened by a successful wife.

I married just such a man at the very start of my career in newspapers but hardly had my career or marriage begun to get off the ground when war halted both.

A fashion artist in wartime had about as much value to a newspaper as a bow and arrow would have had against a jet bomber. When my husband was posted to the Midlands I asked the *Mirror* to release me so that I could become a camp follower. They were very considerate. They'd pay me a small retainer, they said, and I would do any drawings they might want. Meanwhile, I wasn't allowed to work for other newspapers but I could flog sketches to magazines.

I became pregnant and when our son was still an infant, his father departed for distant foreign parts as a soldier with the Royal Engineers and I was not to see him again for almost four years. Before he went away, he installed me and Robert, our baby, in furnished rooms in Stoke Poges in Buckinghamshire, near enough to my parents' pub in Windsor for us to have the comfort of their care and protection.

I slogged away at my fashion drawing, going to London frequently to maintain my contact with the *Mirror*. My agent got me some commissions from the women's magazines but Robert and I were not exactly affluent and the great career I'd dreamed about was stagnant.

Life was dodging bombs, caring for Robert, writing daily to his father in the Far East, watching for his daily letters, trying to bring alive to his small son the hard-to-understand fact for a toddler that the soldier in the photograph was a real person, his far-away father whom he'd see one day. And wondering grimly if he ever would. But I was young and resilient, optimistic and undaunted – like most of that civilian wartime generation – and at night, after Robert was in his cot and the letter written to his father, I'd draw happily away, convinced that the future would be good.

The women's magazines continued to publish and there was a fair amount of work coming my way. Maybe it was cheaper for editors to commission artists than use photographers, but whatever the reasons (and I didn't question them) I was getting a lot of knitwear to sketch. And eye-straining work it was. Every stitch had to be clearly shown, every rib and lacy pattern and cable to be drawn with accuracy, for girls knitting for themselves or for their boy friends had to rely on the sketches to follow their patterns.

One of the editors for whom I did this uninspired work remarked, when I went to deliver, that I wrote very good captions. I thanked her warmly, not having the least idea then what a caption was. Then she asked if I'd written any articles. I said I hadn't and she suggested that since I was a teenage wife and mother living in wartime Britain, I might, perhaps, have a tale or two to tell and how would I like to try my hand at an article of about a thousand words and she'd look at it.

I rushed back to Stoke Poges and wrote a thousand words about the trials of young single-handed motherhood and the editor published it. And commissioned one article a month.

I was a writer. Or so I thought. And when I was invited to write a booklet for distribution to servicewomen about venereal disease, I didn't hesitate to accept. Not that I knew much about it. But I rang a doctor friend in Stoke Poges and asked him if he could give me the low-down on VD. He hesitated and said, somewhat sternly, I thought, that I'd better go round that night after surgery and we'd have a little talk. Clearly, he suspected that I'd been up to something sinister.

He was immensely relieved – and amused – to learn why I needed to know. He gave me some books to read and rather shocked and horrified I began to learn some of the nastier facts of life. I wrote the booklet and started to think about sex as being not quite like the romantic and tender demonstration of marital love I'd always thought it to be.

It may seem curious to the precocious, well-developed, knowing teenagers of today that a young woman of thirty years or so ago could be so limited in knowledge. But some of us led very sheltered sexual lives.

I was still doing fashion drawings for the *Mirror* while all these literary efforts were going on and towards the end of the war in Europe, and a few months before the return of my warrior spouse, came an offer from the *Daily Herald* to join the paper as Fashion Editor, doing the drawings and writing the words.

It was when I joined the *Herald* that I began to realise I wasn't, in fact, a writer. And certainly not a journalist. But I learned and the *Herald* was a great school.

The wartime shortage of any kind of talent meant that available writers were put to full use. I did news stories, covered conferences, wrote features, did book reviews and music criticism. I learned to do subbing and stone-subbing (working on page proofs with the compositors). I covered fashion shows in Paris and Rome and New York and in due course was appointed Woman's Editor . . . the job which finally led to my becoming an advice columnist.

Since those early days, I have been confronted with every possible kind of problem which besets men, women and children. I have dealt with letters written on embossed coroneted notepaper and letters written on tea- and tear-stained scraps. One distraught woman even filled her laundry book with her complex matrimonial problems.

Sometimes the letters are brief and to the point: ('I am fifteen and two months pregnant. Please tell me how to get an abortion right away as I am going on holiday next week.') Others are long, rambling and often almost indecipherable; one letter closely covered seventy-two pages of elderly, sad, spiky writing.

The average daily post adds up to about one hundred letters, though this can fluctuate considerably. If something of specific interest to a large number of readers has appeared in my column in the previous week, this figure can leap into the thousands. Any mention of loneliness, for instance, is guaranteed to swell the mail. If I mention clubs or organisations for getting lonely people together, I know that my staff and I will be coping with an enormous extra load of work.

When I published a letter from a man about how his sexual impotence was driving his wife to seek fulfilment elsewhere and remarked, in my reply, that there were simple techniques he could employ to keep her happy, I was overwhelmed with requests from other men to spell out the techniques to them, too.

A good many people are under the impression that the letters and answers published weekly in the *Mirror* are the beginning and the end of the job. But the five or six letters – selected for publication for their general reader interest – are only the tip of a huge iceberg.

Every reader who writes to me giving an address receives a personal reply and very few, happily, are sent anonymously, though sometimes an urgent and complex problem arrives from someone who says, 'I dare not give you my name and address. Please, please answer in your column.'

If the problem is a particularly intimate one, unsuitable for publication in a national newspaper even in our present explicit climate, I am frustrated by my inability to help those afraid to reveal their identity. Wives of husbands who beat them up, for instance, often say, 'Please do *not* send a reply through the post. If my husband found a letter from you, he would half kill me.' Young, pregnant girls seeking advice about abortions are also among the anonymous writers, scared that a reply from me could reveal their worrying secret to their parents. Many homosexuals, of both sexes, afraid of censure or ridicule, ask anonymously for help via the column.

The managing director of a very well-known company begged me to tell him, in the column, how he could prevent the secretary with whom he'd been having an erotic sexual affair from blackmailing him into continuing the relationship he desperately wanted to end.

With only one page a week in the *Mirror*, space is inadequate to deal with as many of the anonymous letters as I'd like. But luckily, the vast majority of readers send an address. And they get a reply.

The staff of eight dedicated girls who help me with the mammoth task are very carefully chosen for their compassion and expertise, and their interest in the difficulties of other people's lives.

There is a need to be involved and at the same time objective. The first lesson a new adviser in my department receives is the instruction that a letter from a disturbed reader is not simply a few pages setting out the problem. Every letter, I point out, represents a unique human being with what is, to that human being, a unique problem. No matter that fifty similar problems may confront the adviser in the same batch of mail. To the individual reader, the problem is his or hers alone.

I ask my staff to try to visualise the reader as a person, to imagine the circumstances and conditions of his or her life, to reflect on the character of the individual and on those characters – their wives or husbands or children or parents – who may perhaps in some way be responsible or contributory to the problem. For instance, if a wife writes to complain about the cruel or selfish behaviour of her husband, I ask my girls to consider what kind of a wife she might be and how much they can assess of her own blame in the failure of her marriage. For one of the most frustrating aspects of the job I do is the fact that I see only one side of every problem. I hear the complainant's story. I know nothing about the other side of the coin. And it's all too easy to make snap judgements on the basis of very slim evidence.

The staff who help me to deal with letters are supported by several typists and two full-time filing clerks. Filing is a vital part of the operation, for frequently readers become 'cases'. It is sometimes necessary to make a swift reference to previous correspondence.

Occasionally, the police are involved, or organisations like the NSPCC or one of the rescue services like the Samaritans or Alcoholics Anonymous or Age Concern. We also have psychiatrists, psychologists, doctors, lawyers, housing, tax and insurance experts to whom we can refer if necessary for specific information.

I have a close working relationship with Citizens' Advice Bureaux all over the country, with the National Marriage Guidance Council, with children's welfare organisations, the Law Society, the Campaign for Homosexual Equality, the British Medical Association, the Social Services Departments, the Probation Service, the Salvation Army and the police. Plus various religious organisations. Plus individual doctors who sometimes advise their patients to get in touch with me.

We spend almost as much time on the telephone getting answers to readers' questions as we do in replying to their letters and it is not at all unusual to make half a dozen calls to assist one reader.

We have from time to time arranged domiciliary visits to lonely old people, found pen friends, put people in touch with lost relatives, helped people to get their own do-it-yourself divorces, organised wedding receptions, planned parties, assisted with adoptions and saved several lives. It is a fearful responsibility and I am constantly aware of it.

It is not possible to know if those who owe their lives to our prompt action have lived to be grateful but the fact remains that prompt action has been taken on several occasions. On one of these a girl rang me from a telephone box in Notting Hill to say she'd taken most of the contents of a bottle of sleeping pills. While I tried desperately to keep her talking and conscious, so that I could extract from her the exact location of the phone box and her name and address, I was buzzing furiously on the other phone on my desk for 'urgent sos', which is part of the pre-planned drill in such situations.

Sue Tranter, my personal assistant, and Maureen Escott, my secretary, know exactly what to do. They get the police on the other line while I write down as many details about the caller as I can get, which they then convey to the police. With luck, we get enough information for the police to move fast. In this case, they moved very fast indeed and the girl was picked up, unconscious, and rushed to hospital where, it was later reported to me, she was saved.

A desperate wife recently rang me from her home with a similar story of an overdose and we were able to get the police and an ambulance to her and also to arrange for her schoolgirl daughter to be met from school to avoid submitting the child to the shock of going home to find the place in a shambles and her mother fighting for her life in hospital.

I have found the police enormously co-operative in cases of incest where a father, for instance, is reported to me as being suspected of having sexual relations with a young daughter. There's no question of a large flat-footed copper in uniform stomping down to the front door to investigate. Instead, on getting the relevant information, the police will make discreet enquiries.

On one occasion, a woman wrote to me expressing fears about an elderly man who lurked around a park near a school. She'd seen him talking to little girls and offering them sweets and she was afraid that small children might be in danger. I rang the local police and read her letter to them. They arranged for the man to be watched and maintained their vigilance over a considerable period until they were convinced that the elderly man was simply a harmless, lonely old boy who loved kids and was in no way a threat to their safety.

Readers who fear for the safety of children frequently phone or write asking me to get in touch with the NSPCC, not wanting it to be known that they have been spying on neighbours or even relatives who might be neglecting or ill-treating children. The NSPCC are as careful and discreet as the police in investigating such cases.

Occasionally, people with problems arrive at the office, hoping to be able to discuss their troubles but I do not encourage personal visits, which require an entirely different kind of counselling to that which I customarily do. For one thing it is immensely time-consuming. I can reply to as many as fifty letters in a day while, if I saw people for personal consultations, I would be able to cope with no more than half a dozen at most. And my training and experience are geared more to letter-answering than to consultations.

I am frequently asked if many letters are hoaxes. Of course

some are. It's all part of the national sport of taking the rise out
of advice columnists. Students do it. School kids do it. Workers
in their tea breaks do it. Soldiers in the Mess do it.

And it's not too difficult to spot the hoaxes, for the problems
are usually very well thought-out and are highly convoluted and
imaginative. And the writing and composition of the letters is
beautifully neat, with paragraphs, semi-colons and colons and all
the commas and full stops in the right places.

Genuine letters of distress have few full stops and commas,
let alone colons and semi-colons. A disturbed person's writing
reflects that person's disturbed state of mind.

But when the obvious hoax letters arrive, I usually reply to
them unless I am so pressed by desperate and urgent genuine
ones that to spend time writing to hoaxers would be depriving
those in real need of help.

I tell the hoaxers that I suspect they're playing the national
game of mickey-taking and I don't mind really, if writing to me
gave them a giggle or occupied a boring half hour. And just in
case I guessed wrong and their problem *was* a genuine one, I
apologise and suggest a possible solution to the problem. Many
a shamefaced citizen has written back to apologise. And
subsequently written again with an honest problem.

One of the more rewarding aspects of the job is the regular
maintenance of correspondence, sometimes over years. One
reader has been corresponding with me for nearly eighteen
years – not because in all that time I was unable to help her, for
the original reason for her first letter has long since been forgotten by both of us. She is now a lonely lady, severely arthritic
and housebound. She has become an old friend, with pictures of
me and of my family on her mantelpiece. She has my son's
wedding picture and snaps of my grandchildren. She remembers
my birthday. We exchange gifts at Christmas. And if either one
of us is a bit tardy with our letter-writing, we check on each
other anxiously to make sure all is well.

But most of my steady regular correspondents write to maintain contact during the period of major worries in their lives.
For instance, the husband of a well-known singer wrote every
week for months while he was trying, with my support, to

prevent his marriage from breaking up. He needed to write, he said, to keep up his spirits and his resolution. He needed someone to lean on during this traumatic and painful period. He wanted reassurance. He wanted to be given hope that his efforts could succeed.

I believed there was hope and I tried to give him the necessary back-up and though neither he nor I can be certain that the marriage will survive the signs are strong that it will. He no longer writes as often as he did, which is a good sign, and he is very optimistic now, much more in control of the situation and of himself. My fingers are crossed for a contented, if not ecstatically happy ending to this story.

Remembering the successful endings to human dramas underlines the worthwhile aspect of a job which can at times seem utterly unrewarding. For only a comparatively small proportion of people write back and say 'You helped me' or 'Your advice was useful'. Rarely do I learn the end of the story – whether the ending was happy or sad.

Perhaps one of the most difficult and, in the end, the most satisfactory of all my 'cases' was that of a seventeen-year-old boy whose brief and matter-of-fact letter arrived late one Friday evening. He stated the facts quite baldly. He was, he said, an in-patient in a psychiatric ward of a big North of England hospital and he was desperately in love with one of his nurses, who was unable to return his love. Unless he could somehow make this nurse love him, he intended to kill himself. He had finally made up his mind to do this. Could I please advise him, he asked. As an afterthought, he mentioned that the nurse was a married man with two children.

Many people in trouble talk of suicide. 'My life isn't worth living,' say wives whose husbands go to watch soccer Saturday afternoons or spend three evenings a week at the pub. 'I feel like ending it all,' write girls whose boy friends give them a bad time.

Such threats cannot be lightly ignored. But when a mental patient writes in these terms, it's wise to take swift action and I began to dial the phone number of that Northern hospital almost before I got to the end of the letter. I asked if it was possible for me to speak to the psychiatrist in charge of the boy's case and luckily he was available.

I read the letter to him and he was grateful and said extra precautions would be taken. He also expressed surprise at the boy's revelation to me, about which the doctor had no previous knowledge. 'Do you intend to reply?' he asked. 'Certainly,' I said, 'unless you, in charge of his case, advise against it.'

We agreed that I would draft a reply and ring him back to check that it couldn't be harmful to his patient. So I prepared a draft, which the psychiatrist approved, and I promised to let him know if the boy wrote again.

The boy wrote within a week and again I rang his doctor, drafting a further reply for approval. He made one or two valuable suggestions to augment what I'd written and I sent this second letter to the boy. And so the correspondence continued over weeks and months – with every letter from me vetted by the doctor.

The boy revealed much more of his anguish and insecurity to me than he did in talks to his psychiatrist. I became, almost, a substitute mother. And through the frank and revealing letters the boy wrote to me, his doctor was able to help him.

The happy ending to this story was when the doctor finally rang me to say that the boy was so far recovered that he'd been able to take a part-time job and there was every reason to hope for a full recovery in time.

You can chalk up the successes and feel considerable satisfaction doing an absorbing job that can be so rewarding. The failures, though, are unknown and imponderable. You do your best and hope that it works.

Many people ask me if I am, by now, shock-proof.

No. I am not. I am continually shocked and horrified, not by the kind of problems people present (like the hysterical woman who rang to say she'd found her husband having intercourse with their dog), but by the treatment people mete out to each other.

I am freshly shocked by every new demonstration of human cruelty and persecution. It is impossible to shrug off child-battering and wife-beating. It is shocking to me to hear of the persecution of homosexuals or transvestites or others among us who do not conform to the common notion of normality. Revenge and deep-seated spite also shock me, as does hatred. I am shocked by actions perpetrated in the name or the cause of love which bring anguish to others.

But I am not in the least bit shocked by sexual deviations, by pathetic fetishists or by the odd and often unsavoury habits in which some citizens indulge for any variety of sad reasons.

I am mainly shocked by the uncompromising and uncharitable attitudes which the smug and self-satisfied demonstrate towards their less fortunate fellow men and women.

Since I first began to do this job all those years ago on the *Herald*, I've seen a good many changes in the type of problems which beset people.

There have been radical changes in society which have dramatically affected relationships and the most marked, I think, are those which have influenced the attitudes of women.

At the beginning of my career as an adviser, the majority of women regarded themselves as chattels and were regarded thus by men. It was commonplace to receive letters from wives saying 'My husband expects me to *submit* to him once – or twice – or a dozen times a week.' That word 'submit' became one of the dirtier words in my private list of dirty words. Women described themselves as 'mere housewives' and 'mere' went on the dirty word list, too.

In my more despairing moments, I believed that women, cast by society and by themselves into this second-class submissive slave role, would never see that they could and should claim and enjoy equality of status, with just rights as equal citizens and rights to an entitlement of fulfilment at any level. But during the past twenty or so years, the picture has altered. The hated word 'submit' has happily vanished and is crossed off the list. 'Mere' is still on it, but only just and I prophesy that 'mere', too, will disappear entirely before long.

Twenty years ago, women wrote about their sexually demanding men. Now, many men write about sexually demanding women. Aggrieved women ask why they don't get an adequate number of orgasms. If, way back in the *Herald* days I'd had a letter from a woman asking how her man's technique can be improved to ensure her satisfactory orgasms, I'd have fainted dead away on the office floor. Now, questions about orgasms are as commonplace as complaints about mothers-in-law.

There's been no change there. The in-law ogre is still seen as a major threat to marriage, along with classic and traditional meanness, neglect and infidelity, which are the main symptoms – if not the actual causes – of marital breakdowns.

There are more problems relating to children and teenage offspring than there were twenty years ago. The old firm family bonds have weakened; children get out of control, teenagers are wayward and defiant. Words like loyalty, fidelity, trust, discipline and tolerance begin to have an old-fashioned ring. Cynicism and a philosophy based on the 'you've only one life to live – so why not live it up' theme create different problems for today's people, harder problems for advice columnists to solve.

In this book, I have selected samples of problems which have come my way – and my answers to them. They will, perhaps, be helpful to those facing similar problems. Or at any rate, provide some interest for the mild voyeur. For there's no doubt at all (market-research proves it) that most people are fascinated by other people's problems. They're sure they could never happen to them. But daily someone writes, 'Dear Marje, I've been reading your column for years, just for fun. I never thought I'd need to write to you, but after twenty-seven years of marriage to a good, decent husband, I have met another man. . . .'

Marriage: Happy Ever After?

Marriage problems account for about half of the total volume of letters I receive. Of this number, approximately a third come from men.

Ages of correspondents range from brides and grooms of sixteen, to senior citizens whose marriages go on the rocks after perhaps thirty or forty years.

The pattern of marriage has changed perceptibly over the past two decades and the changes have accelerated dramatically in the last decade. People now marry younger, divorce more readily, demand more of their partners at every level: sexual, financial and social. Because their expectations are greater than ever before, the disappointments and frustrations seem also greater.

Power no longer rests with the male as head of the household. The emancipation of women, their demands for equality, their independence of mind and spirit, if not of actual fact, has created a climate in marriage which is, perhaps, the main reason for the changed pattern of the old institution. It is no longer a vehicle for the procreation of children, nor is security – once the aim of every female – the prime reason for marriage. And while romantic love may still bring couples to the altar or the registry office, the old notions of duty and fidelity and responsibility are becoming as obsolete as six-tier wedding cakes. Forever and ever really means as long as it lasts.

But society is still based on the family as a unit. Marriage is as popular as ever it was – even though it disintegrates faster than ever it did. Or appears to. For divorce and separation statistics cannot be a true yardstick for the failures. Many couples now, as in the past, stick it out for various reasons: children, money, possessions, jobs, relatives and religion. Even so present figures indicate that one in four couples marrying now will break their ties in the Divorce Court.

There are three main breakdown peaks. The first is around the fourth year of marriage; the second is at around ten years; the third between twenty and twenty-five years.

Reasons for the very early breakdown of so many marriages often hinge on the failure of high expectations to materialise.

The romantic love which brought couples together becomes increasingly less romantic when the matrimonial home is a bedroom in the parents' already overcrowded house or a couple of squalid rented rooms sharing kitchen and bathroom.

Girls often talk themselves into being madly in love simply to get away from the parental home, only to discover that the fire is a good deal less attractive than the frying pan from which they escaped.

We also know that six out of every ten brides are pregnant at the time of their marriage.

Not all such marriages are shot-gun affairs, for frequently couples have lived together for some time and the pregnancies are planned and the union legalised to legitimise the expected baby. But many young couples marry when the girl becomes accidentally pregnant and these marriages are the ones most at risk.

The highest of all risk marriages are those contracted among teenagers. The youthful husband resents being trapped by marriage: he expects to continue to lead the life he had before, going out with his friends, continuing relationships with other girls. He resents having to spend his earnings on domestic and household needs. When his young wife is forced to give up her job because of her pregnancy, he rebels against having to support her. He neglects her and the home, excludes her from his hobbies and often simply walks out and leaves her after less than a year of marriage.

Quite apart from the complications pregnancies and infants, bad housing and inadequate incomes bring to youthful marriages, many couples soon discover that they are simply incompatible and, whereas in the past they'd have tried to stick it out, today's young couples are inclined to give up without a struggle.

The reasons for the ten-year itch are fairly easy to assess: usually one partner matures more rapidly than the other or develops other involvements and interests. Wives, burdened with small children, become frustrated and irritable. Husbands, struggling with jobs and careers, fail to find refuge and peace in their homes. Tired wives refuse sex. Bored wives demand more of it than hard-working husbands can provide. Communication between the partners breaks down – if it ever existed. Husbands look for comfort or excitement with other women. Wives often take lovers.

They are the marriage drifters, failing to recognise the need to work at the relationship, to grow together and not drift apart.

Marriages which break up after twenty years or more (and they are on the increase) become particularly vulnerable when children have grown up and left home, when the menopausal wife is at a low health-peak, when the middle-aged husband seeks affirmation from other women of his still ripe sexual appeal. These are the couples, mainly, who have stayed together because of the children, because of habit, for easy companion-ship, because they've built up a home and a circle of friends and because there's been no real, tangible reason to separate. They part, usually, when one or other meets a more exciting partner.

I estimate that at least seventy-five per cent of all marriages go through some serious difficulty – serious enough to lead to separation unless the parties make equally serious efforts to resolve their difficulties.

A good many people *do* manage to adjust to their problems, if not to resolve them entirely. Many couples continue to jog along, compromising with an unsatisfactory marriage because it's less complicated to stay together than to part. And, of course, thousands and thousands who face difficulties, great or small, write letters to people like me and await the replies which, they hope, will help them to solve their problems. . . .

Typical of many letters from wives whose marriages suddenly begin to fall apart are these two . . . and my replies.

Q. Six months ago, we were a happy family. We celebrated our Silver Wedding with a lovely party and our children and grandchildren shared our happiness. But within a few weeks, my husband began behaving as he has never behaved in all our married life. He started flirting with other women and I have found out that he's been seeing one woman, much younger than he is, regularly.

I have tackled him, but he lies to me, which has never happened before. I don't know whether he's actually been unfaithful and my life is now plain torture. How can a man suddenly change like this? And why?

A. My guess is that the Silver Wedding celebrations sparked off a sudden flash of realisation. It struck your husband like lightning that he was no longer young and swinging. I am pretty sure this odd and uncharacteristic behaviour is a symptom of his fear of growing old.

Many similarly fearful men cast around desperately for reassurance that age is not withering them. We women do it too, though with women it's inclined to be limited to getting our hair tinted and going on crash diets. We're somewhat less likely to seek our reassurance from young men. But knowing why he does it won't help you to accept with placid equanimity your husband's philandering.

You could try to see it as a kind of sickness from which he'll hopefully recover when he comes to his senses and realises that there's nothing he can do to stop the clock. Or you can make a big effort to swing along with him instead of doing what you probably want to do, which is settle now for calm middle-aged tranquillity.

Difficult as it might be to haul yourself out of a comfortable rut, I think you ought to start competing with the younger opposition. You didn't mention your age, but I estimate that it's likely to be around the fifty mark and that's certainly not too old to grow a bit younger.

Despite his groping around for a younger image himself, I very much doubt if your husband wants to disrupt his marriage and seriously put it at risk. He's reacting, rather than thinking. You'll have to be the thinker of the family at this difficult stage in both your lives. It's not a time for a wife to lose her head.

*

Q. My husband is making us the laughing stock of the neighbourhood.

Things haven't been very good between us for some time. He is forever talking about how life is passing him by, how he's getting old, with nothing to look forward to except bills. He is forty-six and I'm thirty-nine and we have two teenage sons.

A week ago he said he was leaving me. I was very upset at first, but he has moved in with his mother who lives only four doors away and he pops in and out of here frequently. He actually came to watch television last night because his mother's set broke down.

He says he wants time to think about his life. He says, too, that he wants freedom from responsibilities – though his are minimal. I go out to work and he does nothing in the house.

A. What, I wonder, is causing you the most concern: the neighbours laughing their heads off at your spouse and his half-hearted departure? Or his immature attitude to life? Or the fact that he's left you to go back home to his mother? I'm not sure whether you are upset by the loss of your mate – or whether you are aggrieved because he's made you both look foolish.

I'm very puzzled as to why he's taken this step. Most men who leave their wives because they feel restless in middle age, uneasy about the future and tired of their responsibilities which suddenly seem to weigh so heavily, make their departure much more spectacular. The cure for what ails them, they so often figure, is an affair with another woman. Your husband seems to be having an affair with a television set, practically on your doorstep.

Strangely, you do not mention love in your letter, so I have no idea whether you love him and yearn for his return to you and not merely to your TV set. You do not mention sex, either. Perhaps neither love nor sex motivated your marriage, in which case, he may well regard it as a pretty sterile one – hardly worth keeping alive.

If you want him back because you love him, next time he pops in to watch his favourite programme, I suggest you offer him even better entertainment than the box can provide. It shouldn't be beyond your feminine skills to distract him, however good the programme. Then, when he goes back to his mother's house to think, he'll have something worth thinking about and something to look forward to apart from bills and he might decide that he can face up to the responsibilities of marriage for the sake of the pleasant bonus.

But if you regard his desertion as no more than an injury to your pride and a joke for the neighbourhood, it's easy enough to prevent him using you and your house as a convenient alternative to his mother's. Just change the lock on the door and refuse to let him in when he rings the bell. Say, through the letter box, that you're busy. That will certainly give him something to think about.

And I hope I've given you something to think about, too.

Money is the root of much of the evil which attacks marriages and over recent years, problem letters which relate to money have dramatically increased in number.

I am frequently asked to adjudicate in arguments over cash. What proportion of a husband's salary, wives ask, are they entitled to expect?

Women get into debt and often write asking me to lend them cash to tide them over. They tell me they are terrified to reveal to their husbands the extent of unpaid bills. Many husbands are accused of being mean; many wives of being feckless and bad managers.

Women tell me their husbands refuse to believe that household bills can possibly account for the sums women spend. I advise them to make detailed lists of every item they buy over a period of a month and to go through the list with their husbands.

Sometimes husbands will actually pore over the lists with their wives and begin to understand the financial problems which confront so many women.

Wives say they wouldn't mind the struggles so much if only husbands were at least sympathetic.

Ideally, I tell wives, make your husband do the shopping, or at any rate accompany you to the shops. But ideal husbands are thin on the ground. All too many are sadly like this one. . . .

Q. There are rent tribunals, pay boards and ministers keeping an eye on inflation, but what I and many other women need is a housekeeping board to keep an eye on our husbands.

I have to pay every bill out of my housekeeping money. Despite the fact that my husband has recently had two significant wage rises by changing jobs, I've not had an extra penny from him.

I am at my wits' end. I have nothing left at the end of the week for clothes, let alone hairdos or spending money.

With two young children, I don't really want to leave them to go out to work but I may have to get a job.

My husband smokes heavily and goes drinking two or three times a week. He denies himself nothing.

Is there any way I can make him give me an adequate allowance?

A. I advise tough sanctions against husbands like yours.

If a man doesn't give his wife enough cash to enable her to manage, she should keep him short of food. She should let him go hungry to bed. She should refuse to perform normal matrimonial duties, like sewing on his buttons and ironing his shirts. Let him do his own darned ironing.

Women married to such men need feel no sense of guilt for inflicting punishment on them. They deserve what they get.

Any decent wife will do everything she can to contrive to make ends meet when her husband's on low pay. But if a man who benefits from a wage increase neglects to up his wife's allowance, she's entitled to take action.

The trouble is that many women are too timid to take a strong stand.

I don't think you ought to go out to work and neglect your young children simply because this selfish man keeps you short of cash. Why should you make sacrifices so that he can continue to smoke and drink while you and his children suffer?

Get wise and get tough. Neither he nor other husbands like him merit loving consideration.

It must be admitted that a good many women *are* extravagant, *are* bad managers and *do* fail to take into account the fact that with all the will in the world, a man's salary cannot stretch endlessly.

Q. I am worried out of my wits about money. My husband is as generous as he can afford to be and I earn a small wage from a part-time job. But somehow I can never get straight. I'm now in debt to the extent of nearly £150 and I dare not tell my husband. I am terrified in case he finds out and don't know what to do.

A. The first thing you have to do is brace yourself to tell your husband. I know it's a tough job, but it has to be done. Better for you to tell him than for him to find out from someone else – as he probably will.

Wait for the right moment. Don't interrupt him, for instance, when he's watching soccer on TV or rushing to catch his train.

But before you tell him, work out a plan to organise your finances. Self-discipline is the only way to do it.

Spend a bit more on a notebook. Note down your weekly financial commitments and the amount of money you have to meet them. Vow to write down every penny expended – including the smallest items. Don't skip bus fares or that lipstick you couldn't resist. In other words, start a proper book-keeping budget. Show your husband your notebook at

2

the time of the confession so he'll know you really mean to stick to a system and not get in this mess ever again.

If you pick the right moment, there's a very good chance he'll help you out. Help you to keep straight if, with ashes on your head and your head on his shoulder, you ask him to.

A letter from a young wife concerning her husband's financial problems highlights another interesting fact of married life: an astonishingly large number of people marry knowing very little about each other.

In this case, the husband was afraid to reveal his difficulties in case the girl called off the wedding.

Q. We had only been married a week when my husband said he wanted to talk to me seriously. Then he proceeded to knock the breath out of me by confessing that he is heavily overdrawn at the bank and also owes money to his friends. He is about five hundred pounds in debt. He says he was scared that if I knew before the wedding, I'd change my mind.

I feel so shattered and bitter towards him I don't see how our marriage can survive, or why I should help sort out his problem. He promises we will get straight, but how can I trust him again. What do you think I should do?

A. What I think you should do is stop whimpering and get down to working out how you can help your husband sort out his finances.

Of course you're worried. So is he and now that you are married to him, you'd better get used to the idea that pretty well every problem in a marriage can be resolved if there's determination and good will on the part of both partners.

What you should do now is get a job, save like mad and economise until it hurts, until the debts are cleared. And, together, work out a budget and stick to it. If he's the feckless one of the family, you've got to be the careful one. I daresay you've got weaknesses too which, with his help, can be overcome.

Most marriages have to survive crises. You've just been rather unlucky to have to face a major crisis so early on in the game.

The following few letters illustrate several different areas of difficulty which pose a threat to marriage. . . .

Q. My husband's cool attitude towards our baby daughter, born three weeks ago, is upsetting me immensely.

I became pregnant before we were married but we were going to get married anyway, so it wasn't a shot-gun wedding.

I can't understand why my husband seems so disinterested in such a lovely baby. He is loving towards me – but when I ask him if he's pleased with the baby, he just says 'Sure'. But he doesn't pick her up or cuddle her and I am worried in case my baby will suffer because of her father's disinterest.

A. Many men do not find tiny infants as fascinating, beautiful and unique as do their mothers. To you, the baby is a precious miracle. To your husband, she's probably a squawking red-faced disturbance who keeps him awake at nights and deprives him of your total attention towards him.

Wait until your baby daughter becomes aware enough to realise there's a man around the house to twine around her fat little finger. Your husband will be drooling over her and boring everyone with endless stories of her charm and brilliance. Don't press him to admire her now. He'll do it soon enough without the slightest encouragement.

Just take care you don't fall into the well-known old trap that has threatened so many marriages. You may have a lovely baby, but you've also got a husband who just might secretly be jealous of the love he now finds he has to share with an infant. Just watch out that in loving her, you don't withhold any from him.

*

Q. When I got married I was six months pregnant. My daughter is now two years old.

I'd had plenty of boy friends – and sex – before I met my husband and was glad, really, to settle down. We were happy enough during the first few months but the last year has been torture.

He accuses me of sleeping with other men and is suspicious of everything I do. Even when I go shopping there's a cross-examination about who I met. I think he suspects me of sleeping with every tradesman.

I have never looked at another man since I married, but sometimes I feel like starting something just to punish him. It would serve him right if I did.

It is a miserable existence and I am wondering if we ought to part now, while we're both still young enough to start again. What do you think?

A. There's always a big risk attached to shot-gun weddings. It doesn't sound as if yours was based on love and a mutually passionate longing to live together. It appears to have been a practical arrangement to legitimise your baby. Often marriages like yours do work out very well indeed. It depends how much both parties want it to. But if your husband is going to punish you forever for trapping him into marriage (which is probably the reason behind his suspicions) and if you are constantly brooding about punishing him for punishing you, you might as well pack it up now.

There's one thing both of you seem to be forgetting: the punishment you are both handing out to the innocent victim of all this – the baby.

You'd better hold a solemn family council meeting. And set out an agenda, putting right at the top the welfare and future of your daughter. Resolve to stop all the punishment and try for a peaceful settlement. You are both responsible for one small girl who will be better off with two parents than one, provided, of course, those parents can stop their silly bickering and start behaving like sensible adults with a job to do, which is making good a marriage built on pretty frail foundations.

*

Q. When we married, my husband and I decided that we were not going to sacrifice our independence. We felt that by continuing to go out with other people our marriage would not become stale. It was understood that these extra-marital relationships would be platonic and they have been so far as I am concerned, though I'm not so sure about him.

Now, after two years, I wish we were like normal couples. I envy people who seem to need only each other. But when I said this to my husband, he accused me of breaking my promise. He says he loves me – but insists on the freedom we agreed to.

A. Well, it's really hardly a marriage is it? In fact, I can't imagine why you bothered with the legalities or, at any rate, why you allowed yourself to be talked into an arrangement which leaves you both almost as uncommitted as if you were just good friends. For I suspect that the plan for total freedom was promoted more enthusiastically by him than by you.

But your husband is justified in saying you've gone back on your word, for you have. You may have changed your views – but that's no reason why he should change his.

Heaven forbid I should encourage you to give up hope and jump despairingly into bed with someone else. But I think you ought to carry on being friendly with other people. Platonically, I stress. And tell your husband that if he's never going to settle down to the conventional domesticity you crave, it's best to part while you're young enough to find someone on your more mature wavelength.

*

Q. After twelve years of marriage my wife has decided to leave me. She says there is no other man but she is tired of my selfishness.

I know I am in many ways to blame for I have not always been as thoughtful as I could have been. I admit I have neglected her and I have not always been faithful, either, but I love my wife deeply and would do anything to get my marriage together again.

Would it be possible for you to write to her for me and try to convince her I love her and will spend the rest of my life making her happy if only she'll give me another chance?

A. I'd like to oblige, but my unbreakable rule is never to write to people unless they ask for help or advice.

I sympathise with you, of course. And with her. And I won't heavily underline the obvious, though I must mention it in passing. You've woken up, very late in the day, to the fact that you've been a pretty unsatisfactory husband.

There are a good many men like you, I'm afraid. Some wives stick it out, lacking, perhaps, the courage or the self-confidence to break away and make a new, independent life for themselves.

Life is a bit easier these days for women. They can get jobs and manage to support themselves and though sometimes they settle for a much lower standard of living, they'd rather do that than remain enslaved to selfish and unfaithful husbands.

I don't know how you can convince your wife that you regret past sins of omission and commission. You could write to her yourself, as frankly and as honestly as you wrote to me. You could beg for another chance to prove you mean what you write.

I hope she will give you another chance and that if she does you'll grasp at the opportunity to show her in deeds, as well as fine words, that your remorse is genuine and your intentions unshakeable. But hurt and angry women, I must warn you, take a hell of a lot of convincing.

Marriage: A Kind of Contest?

By far the largest numbers of letters I receive from married people are to do with the sexual problems which beset them. These can be the cause of a marriage breakdown. Or the effect.

People use sex as a punishment or they withhold it as a punishment. They use it as a tool of blackmail, as an inducement, as an award. They endure it, bargain with it, lie about it, joke about it, boast about it, avoid it, are obsessed by it or disgusted by it.

They are, at any rate, a good deal less secretive about it than they used to be, which is healthy. For if people are ready – and able – to discuss their sexual problems frankly with an expert, there is a very good chance that they can be helped to overcome the difficulties they face in their marriages.

I am gratified that so many men and women feel that they can frankly expose their most intimate problems to me and that the years of study of sexual psychology and sexual difficulties have made it possible for me to give help when people so urgently cry out for it.

Many years ago, I came to the conclusion that so far as I am concerned, euphemisms are out. I write explicitly to my readers, using words which they themselves would use if their inhibitions didn't prevent them from expressing themselves in frank terms, and on-going correspondence with readers experiencing sexual difficulties shows that while, at the beginning of the correspondence, they may be reluctant to use explicit language, they feel encouraged to do so by the tone and style of my letters to them as time goes on.

The importance of good sex in marriage cannot, of course, be minimised. But from experience based on the huge correspondence relating to it, I am disturbed by the modern tendency to overestimate its importance and by what I regard as the wrong emphasis all too often placed on it by psychologists and counsellors.

Marriage can work perfectly well when sex is not copy-book perfect. Too many sex manuals read by too many gullible people have led them to believe that unless sex is always at a high peak of ecstasy and total fulfilment, it is a failure. I do not subscribe to this view. If it happens thus, it is a bonus. If it does not, it is not necessarily a disaster.

People have been encouraged to expect such perfection, such expertise that those who fail to achieve it can only feel a powerful and damaging sense of failure.

The modern approach to sex has made it seem one of achievement. It has become a technology, a test, a performance, a kind of contest instead of a demonstration and culmination of love and tenderness and emotion.

Which is not to say that technique is to be disregarded. But techniques without love, passion without tenderness, performance without emotion leave one or both of the participants with the feeling that, while the contest may have been won with equal scores to both, the missing factor of mutual affection leaves a dissatisfaction that is far deeper than the physical dissatisfaction of unfulfilled sex.

Sometimes I use a cooking analogy when writing to wives over-anxious about their sexual expertise. I explain that five out of six times, a woman manages to prepare a meal that is satisfactory to the appetite, if not quite up to cordon bleu standards. On the sixth occasion, she'll be inspired to produce something memorable and altogether rewarding and married sex is something like this. Or it ought to be.

If perfection is achieved more often, it's all to the good. But as long as appetites are assuaged and no one goes hungry, there isn't a lot of reason to complain.

Many women have written back to say that this analogy is comforting and puts the whole thing into sensible proportions, for over-anxiety about sexual performance brings in its wake a growing sense of inadequacy and inferiority, of jealousy and doubt which eats away at the very foundations of the marriage.

One of the difficulties people face is that because they have become aware, either sharply or vaguely, that high standards of expertise are desirable, they have no way of measuring their own standards. A letter from an uncertain young wife illustrates this dilemma. . . .

Q. Do you think my husband is undersexed? We make love only three or four times a month and it seems to me that this isn't very often for people of our age (we are both twenty-one) who have been married for exactly fourteen months.

Before I was married, I had a very virile boy friend. It was every possible night with him.

Don't think, please, that I feel upset or deprived or anything, for I'm not really very sexy myself and certainly do not feel starved of sex or love. My husband is very loving. I just wondered if he ought to see a doctor in case there's something wrong.

A. You cannot measure sexuality with a yardstick. There aren't any rules or standards by which you can judge whether or not a person is undersexed or oversexed or merely average. People's sex drives vary as widely as do their other appetites. Some eat hearty meals three times a day; others keep healthy and happy on a comparatively meagre diet.

The important factor is that lovers should, as far as possible, be matched in their desires. You are falling into the trap of comparing your husband with your former boy friend who may or may not have continued at his earlier pace if you'd married him. He might well by now be down to the once a week level. Once a man and woman get married, the domestic pressures build up. There's a home to run and bills to pay and distracting responsibilities.

As long as neither of you feels frustrated, as long as the sexual needs of both of you are fulfilled, you have nothing to worry about – and certainly no problem to bother the doctor with.

2*

The years of middle age can be a difficult period for women, sexually. Many tell me they think that middle-aged sex is somehow rather nasty. Some consider it to be disgusting and their rejection of their still virile husbands at this time of their lives often drives men to seek consolation and reassurance from younger women.

Q. After eighteen years of a happy and sexually good marriage, my wife has lately become much less enthusiastic about love-making than she was.

She was always quite uninhibited and sex was fun, with no nonsense about when or where. But now, she wants to wait until bedtime, insists that the lights be put out and is altogether behaving in a strangely uncharacteristic way.

I can think of no explanation and she won't talk about it. She is forty-five and I am wondering if it has anything to do with the menopause and if, in your experience, you've come across similar cases and what you advise.

A. Some women do lose their interest in sex during the menopausal period, but women who have always been enthusiastic usually continue to be, unless, of course, there is a physical reason behind their reluctance, which only a doctor could diagnose.

One possible explanation occurs to me. As middle age creeps up on a woman, she sometimes puts on weight. She looks – or thinks she looks – less attractive and desirable. She is almost certain to have acquired a few wrinkles and bulges.

Perhaps your wife has noticed she no longer has the youthful bloom which can stand up to observation in a harsh light. In other words, she'd prefer you not to see her – and notice for yourself the changes that mark the end of her youth. Understandable, and very human.

If you want her to lose her new self-consciousness, keep on telling her you find her even more beautiful as the years go by. Sing the praises of a rounded, mature body. Emphasise your delight in her curves – and I think your reassuring praise will soon have all the lights blazing away again.

I am never surprised to have letters from people – mostly women – who tell me that sex for them is distasteful or disgusting, for despite our more enlightened approach to it today, there's still a hangover of deep guilt among many who have been conditioned to believe that sex is dirty. It is a hangover produced by mothers who told their young daughters that anything to do with genitals is either very private or exceedingly nasty.

Mothers who smack toddlers found masturbating are responsible for many of the sexual problems their children face in adult life, producing feelings of deep guilt about sex, especially about the enjoyment of sex. People write to me telling me of these guilts. They are afraid of enjoyment, afraid of exposing feelings of pleasure and excitement, afraid, even, to touch the genitals of their partners. And in a climate where they feel that a high level of sexual expertise is expected of them, they see themselves as inadequate failures and their marriages are put at great danger by their fears and unnecessary guilts.

Q. I love my husband deeply but sex to me simply intrudes on a happy relationship. I do it for my husband's sake, but experience nothing myself.

He has patiently put up with the situation until now, but we have been married six years and I think the strain is at last beginning to tell. He has started making some pointed and cruel remarks and I realise that if I am going to save my marriage, which I desperately want to do, I must somehow change.

Am I abnormal, do you think? And have I left it too late to try to improve matters? We are both in our thirties and have one daughter.

A. I am not going to be able to tell you how to turn overnight into a sex-hungry woman. But the fact that you want so desperately to be able to respond to your husband is a good start.

There's no clue in your letter as to why you are disinterested in sex. But it's interesting and encouraging that you do not appear to have an actual revulsion to it. That's harder to deal with than what seems to be mere indifference.

Most people deeply in love regard sex as a culmination of their relationship. It is part of a lover's desire to give, to possess and to be possessed in physical as well as emotional terms. In the close intimacy of love-making there is constant renewal of love in the context of passion. And it's only now, when you feel that your marriage is threatened, that you begin to recognise the immense importance of this part of marriage.

You ask if I think that you are abnormal. I doubt it. If you were, I imagine you'd let your marriage go and feel thankful not to have to bother about sex any longer.

Have you left it too late? you ask. I do not think so. But you might need professional help, an analysis which could trace the reasons for your lack of sexuality. There may be some long-forgotten incident in your childhood which put you off sex or some deep guilt about it buried in your sub-conscious mind which needs to be released before you can participate fully and happily.

Ask your doctor to put you in touch with someone expert in this field. But before you go to these lengths, think about love and passion, about giving and receiving. Think about the pain you inflict on the man you love when you allow him reluctant access to your body. Think about the pleasure both of you miss and have missed for so long.

Ask him to tell you where to touch him and how. Tell him to touch you, to play with your body with hands and tongue. Arrange to have 'touching' sessions without necessarily ending them with intercourse unless you both need it.

There are certain extra-sensitive areas of the body, known as the erogenous zones, which, when caressed, stimulate sexual desire. In women, these areas are usually the genitals, inside the thighs, the breasts and nipples, buttocks and lower part of the back. But other parts of the body are sensitive to stimulation, too. The ears, for instance, when they are gently touched or lightly kissed.

Finding the most sensitive erogenous areas is a matter for each individual, a matter of experiment. Try touching your own body and guiding your husband to those areas which cause excitement and create the lubricating genital flow which demonstrates that you are aroused. Think about your body and his as objects of mutual enjoyment.

Take your time, both of you. Be patient. You cannot expect to become proficient overnight in new skills and sex is a skill and an art which lovers can learn to perfect. Put those six wasted years behind you and begin, now, to look forward to guilt-free enjoyment and I am sure your husband's cruel remarks will disappear forever.

Then there are a good many wives who find sex boring or participate out of a sense of wifely duty. . . .

Q. Perhaps it's because I'm forty-three, but sex doesn't interest me these days. I never did find it exciting, but now, to be honest, I find it boring.

Of course I wouldn't tell my husband the real truth for I love him and I don't want to make him feel inadequate. But I did hint to him that I hadn't been feeling very well lately and that love-making was a bit of a strain. I told him that if he agreed to restrict it to once a week I would be willing to let him have sex.

Instead of being understanding he was very annoyed and he hasn't approached me since. That was two months ago. Now I'm worried that he might have another woman and that would be more than I could bear.

A. I'll be glad to advise you for you are surely heading for disaster. Your boredom with sex is pathetic and your age is neither reason nor excuse for it.

At forty-three, you should be at the top of your sexual form, eagerly looking forward to love-making instead of restricting your husband to a once-a-week ration. It's a wonder you haven't issued him with coupons.

Seriously – and it is indeed a serious matter – you must try to discover why sex has always been so unexciting.

I'll make a few guesses so as you can see if I'm anywhere near the mark.

I suspect you've either never or only very rarely reached a climax. I suspect that you've regarded love-making as one of your domestic duties, like cooking and ironing. I suspect that you have allowed your husband his 'rights' instead of participating in mutual enjoyment.

Another possibility occurs to me: your husband, like many men, may not know the technique for arousing you and waiting until you are ready. He may not know how to give you the fulfilment that makes sex between a loving couple so indescribably rewarding for both. He could be ignorant. Or selfish.

Both of you may be and probably are, totally unadventurous, making sex a regular habit like brushing teeth and just about as exciting, sticking to the same old position. It's terrible to think what you've been missing all these boring years.

If any of the guesses I've made seem to you possible reasons for your disinterest, I may have helped you to start improving the situation.

Certainly, if you think your husband is not playing his part, you must help him to, by word and guidance. And for goodness sake, lift the sanctions you've imposed. If he's so cross that he won't approach you, then you must approach him. Give him a lovely surprise. Be bold and you'll soon stop being bored.

You are right to be concerned that he might start approaching someone else. I expect he will unless you remove the rationing system you've imposed. We've all got enough shortages. There shouldn't ever be a shortage of love.

It is curious that although, when women are questioned about their sexual fantasies, they often freely admit to having them, many are shocked when they discover that their husbands also fantasise and use their colourful fantasies to promote sexual enjoyment.

Women write distressed letters about discovering caches of

girlie magazines in husbands' garden sheds or hidden behind suits in wardrobes. One wife told me of her horror at finding a number of erotic publications in her husband's filing cupboard, usually kept locked, which he'd carelessly left open one morning when he went to work. (Did he, I wonder, leave it unlocked 'accidentally on purpose' so that she could discover his private reading matter?)

I have had to reassure countless wives who believed their husbands were kinky or debased because they learned of the fantasies which turned their men on to sex.

Q. I don't really know how to explain this to you, but I'll try. I have been happily married for twenty years and we have two sons. Our sex life has always been satisfactory though pretty routine, I'll admit.

Recently my husband seems to have changed in a curious way. Some of the things he has asked me to do lately seem quite bizarre, like making love to me when I am wearing undies and not in bed but on the floor, for instance. There are other things, too. He wants to make love when I am wearing a suspender belt. And last night he suggested I should wear only a bra and high-heeled shoes.

I must confess to feelings of shock and I feel guilty about condoning something which seems so unusual and somehow debased, particularly at our age. I am three years younger than my husband.

Why do you suppose he has suddenly changed like this – and do you think I should encourage his behaviour or try to curb it?

A. It is a little difficult to understand why a man who appears to have been pretty unimaginative in bed for so many years has suddenly developed the exotic tastes you describe. But I do not think, really, that the reasons for his new approach to sex matter quite so much as your reactions to it. There is probably some quite simple explanation – like a friend at the office or someone he's met in a pub saying that when a man reaches middle age is the time for him to liven up his sex life while he's still capable of enjoying it. Which is good thinking.

My thinking on the subject is that it doesn't matter what lovers get up to – as long as they love each other and as long as neither is offended or revolted or upset by the demands or the behaviour of the other.

You feel guilty, you say, about *condoning* something unusual. Wouldn't it be better for you both if you started thinking more constructively? You sound more puzzled than put off. Perhaps, in fact, you secretly rather enjoy this new-style love-making and if you do, there is no reason on earth why you shouldn't shed those unnecessary guilty feelings and relax and join in the fun.

I hope you *can* relax and become as enterprising as he is – for the sad fact is that a good many husbands, scared of indulging their sexual fantasies with their lady wives, all too often seek other, less inhibited partners.

Wives who try to curb their husbands' adventurous antics have no one but themselves to blame if their men hunt for women with a similarly adventurous spirit. And believe me, they're not hard to find.

*

Q. I have never had any worries about our sex life before. My husband is loving, considerate and very passionate. But the other night he really shocked me and since then I have felt unsure of his love.

I asked him what he thought about during love-making. He admitted that he often invented fantasies and some which were very strange and erotic. He said he would never actually act out any of his fantasies, but thinking of them helped to get him excited and enjoy intercourse more.

He really made me feel inadequate, though I have always responded and often make the advances.

Is it normal for men to think about such things when making love?

A. Perfectly normal – and entirely acceptable, so you can stop worrying.

Most men – and women – have interesting and erotic sexual fantasies which arouse their passions. These fantasies certainly do not mean that their love for their partners is in any way diminished.

Think about the men who get kicks from looking at pin-up pictures or thumbing through girlie magazines. You surely cannot believe that every man who does this is in love with a photo of a busty blonde instead of being in love with his wife.

Eroticism without love is pretty debased, but when two people love each other, anything that helps to excite and arouse them is good for them.

I shouldn't imagine for a moment that you are inadequate or that he thinks you are. I think you must be very adequate indeed and advise you to share his fantasies, enjoy them and the mutual benefits they bring.

I am frequently asked by both men and women if I believe that group sex or wife and husband swopping can revitalise a flagging marital relationship. Psychiatrists' opinions are divided. Some believe that group sex or a change of partners can be therapeutic; others that it is fishing in very dangerous waters and I share the latter opinion.

I have received many letters from men and women who have made these kind of experiments, with disastrous results to their marriages, and not one letter which described them as a success.

It can be argued that contented people do not write to advice columnists and by and large this is true, although I do, from time to time, hear from people who tell me that their marriages are good or are now working well after a bad patch. Just the same, I do not subscribe to the view that an ailing relationship can be revived by group-sex methods and when people ask whether I think they should try this method of survival, I warn them of what I see as the likely consequences. . . .

Q. My husband and I met another couple around our age (late twenties) at a party last year. The outcome of this meeting was regular wife-swopping sessions to which we all readily agreed.

But the other wife has told me privately that she hates it and is very unhappy and she has asked me to co-operate in stopping it.

But I enjoy making love to her husband and I know he wants to go on with it and so does my husband. So should I agree to do what she wants or is she being selfish in spoiling fun for the other three?

A. I wouldn't want to advise anyone to stop doing something they regard as fun. But I do not believe that couple-swopping enriches marriages, or aids ailing ones. I believe that it can be the dangerous path which leads to final disaster – if not for all four parties, at least for some.

Already one of your group is suffering. Already one marriage is threatened.

The other wife is probably at the point of refusing to make love to your husband and I wouldn't blame her. If it revolts her, I can see no reason why she should submit to such an intimate activity just to please the rest of the group. Furthermore, your husband isn't likely to continue to enjoy sex with a woman who hates it. And then what? That will leave just two of you – you and the other husband.

I can foresee very dangerous situations arising out of this fun foursome and none of them funny. If you want to preserve your own marriage, let alone your friends' marriage, you will pull out before both sets of marriages are wrecked.

*

Q. A girl with whom I've been very friendly since we were teenagers visits me and my husband regularly. I have been married for two years and she is single. I know my husband finds her attractive but I have never minded because I'm so fond of her but I was utterly shocked when he laughingly suggested – and she laughingly agreed – that it would be fun for all three of us to go to bed together for what he described as a romp.

I was furious but my husband said I was an idiot to take it seriously. Just the same, I have an idea he meant it seriously and now I don't know what to do. Should I forbid her to come to my house?

A. I certainly think you'd be wise to cool this friendship. It seems in danger of getting out of hand. But at this stage of the game, I wouldn't do anything so dramatic as forbidding her ever to cross your threshold again. Just arrange for her visits to be less regular and more infrequent but act casually and don't make a big song and dance about it, either to her or to your husband.

If he laughingly brings up the subject again, laugh along with him and in your jokiest way tell him it's really a very unfunny idea and highly explosive to a happy marriage.

The most sensible thing you could do is hunt around for a single man to pair up with your girl friend. Just be wary, though, in case your husband suggests, in his happy laughing way, that four in a bed might be more fun than just two. You've got to be watchful with this high-spirited man of yours and make it plain that you are not in favour of games which more than two can play.

What is natural? What is normal? What should I allow my husband to do to me? How far should I go in acceding to his sexual demands? These are constantly recurring questions in my mail, demonstrating, once again, the problems people face when communication between them is sparse or non-existent, when they cannot find words to express to each other their doubts and fears and need a third party to allay those fears or help them to face up to their problems.

Q. I remember you once stated that any sexual practice between a husband and wife is permissible, provided it's not objectionable to either one. Well, in my marriage, the things

my husband expects of me are unnatural and absolutely
intolerable. They include oral sex and entry from behind.

We have been married only a year and I don't know how
to face the future. I have tried talking to him but he says I am
a puritan at heart, which is not true, and continues to insist
on practices I find disgusting. I am becoming quite ill over it
all.

At first when he behaved what I consider normally, everything was fine and I loved him.

My parents are elderly and wouldn't understand if I talked
of them and my doctor is not the sort of man I could possibly
go to with this problem. Can you please advise me?

A. No woman is bound, either by law or by duty, to submit to
sexual practices which are unnatural or which revolt her to
such a degree that her health suffers. The law, in fact,
protects her when protection is necessary.

You say your marriage started well, that at the beginning
you loved your husband. I note the past tense. It is clear the
love has vanished. Whether or not there is a chance it could
be revived is problematical. I think it depends on him. If he
cannot be persuaded to change his sexual habits, you are
going to become more and more sickened by them, although
I must tell you many couples enjoy oral sex.

I am not very optimistic about him, but if he'd agree to
seek help, there could be some hope for your marriage. It is a
pity you are unable to discuss the problem fully with him and
are reluctant to discuss the situation with your doctor.
Perhaps it would be easier for you to see a woman doctor. You
could consult one privately. The post office will have a list.
Or you could see one at a Family Planning Clinic. But I
doubt if this would help much unless your husband would
agree to go with you and talk the whole matter out frankly.

You could try this approach as a last ditch-effort to save
the marriage. But unless he is willing to co-operate, and if he
still demands practices which revolt you, the best thing you
could possibly do is leave him while you are still young
enough to fall in love again.

*

Q. I recently remarried after being a widow for four years. My first marriage was humdrum, especially as far as the sexual side was concerned. My husband's demands were no more than perfunctory, which is perhaps the reason why my new husband's attitude to this side of our marriage has startled and, to be truthful, shocked me. He expects me to participate in what I can only describe as erotic practices in very strange positions and circumstances.

I'm not suggesting that he is perverted but I am shy and reserved and do not know how to cope, nor whether I should do things which I've never done before. Yet I love him desperately and want my marriage to succeed.

I am thirty-nine and he is forty-four and was a bachelor when we married a month ago.

A. Your new husband probably assumes that a woman who had been married before knows all the answers and all the sexual tricks. I think the best way to cope with what is, for you, a totally new way of sex, is to tell him frankly that, despite your previous marriage, you are quite inexperienced – a mere child, at thirty-nine, at playing the love game. Ask him to be patient, to go easy, to teach you to enjoy fulfilled love-making, for if you feel you are being driven to participate in practices which alarm or disturb you, you are certainly going to be resistant to them.

From what you say, there is nothing sinister in your husband's love-making. All you need is encouragement to be more relaxed, more ready to experiment and to see sex as a great part, though not, of course, the only important part, of a great marriage. I think that if you can do this, you will soon begin to share pleasures you never dreamed were possible in the old days and your new marriage will be the success you so long for it to be.

One of the most serious sexual problems which can beset a marriage is when the husband is unable to control his climax.

Countless men who suffer from premature ejaculation have asked me if there is any way they can be helped, and letters on this subject are on the increase. I put this down to the fact that although it is certainly no new problem for men, more and more wives today expect satisfaction and make it plain to their husbands that premature ejaculation leaves them deeply frustrated.

In the past, I assume, women put up with this state of affairs without complaint. Or if they *did* complain, husbands had no way of seeking help or no inclination to seek it. In today's frank climate, men are no longer so reluctant to ask for advice. Whenever I have published a letter from a man with this problem, hundreds more with the same problem have written for help.

Q. Every time I make love to my wife I ejaculate as soon as I enter her. We have not been married long and as you can imagine I feel deeply embarrassed. She gets no satisfaction at all and I know she thinks me a failure at love-making.

Before we married, our love-making was always rather hurried, so it didn't matter when I climaxed quickly. I am afraid that if nothing can be done to help me, my marriage will be in danger.

A. Many men suffer from premature ejaculation at some time. It is particularly common in young men, who tend to get very excited and quickly stimulated.

It is possible you may be able to delay your climax by lying still and thinking of anything which will take away your attention long enough for your excitement to die down. Unlikely as it may seem, some men work out mathematical problems at such moments; others ponder their football coupons.

Wearing a condom or even two reduces sensation and makes it easier to delay climax, though this is obviously not a good solution.

There is a treatment you can try for yourself with the help of your wife. It has a high success rate and is used in sex therapy clinics: your wife should stimulate your penis by hand until you feel you are near to climaxing; then tell her to stop and wait until your excitement has subsided. She should repeat the stimulation and again you should tell her to stop just before climax. Make sure you don't leave it too late to signal her to stop. If you do – don't worry, just try again later.

By your wife repeatedly bringing you almost to the point of orgasm and then stopping, you should be able to control ejaculation.

When you are able to do this, your wife should squat over you while you lie on your back. She then puts your penis into her vagina and stimulates it gently, stopping in just the same way when you are about to reach climax. When your excitement has subsided she must begin again, repeating the exercise until you feel you can control ejaculation for as long as you want.

You might like to try an additional method known as the 'Masters and Johnson squeeze technique'. They discovered that a wife can rapidly decrease her husband's sexual urge by squeezing the rim below the top of the penis each time he is about to climax. But you may find this uncomfortable; not everyone who tries this technique finds that it is suitable for him.

One of the commonest female sexual disfunctions which I am called upon to deal with is 'frigidity'. I deliberately put frigidity in quotation marks because it is widely accepted that except in the rarest of cases, there is no such thing as a frigid woman. Many women are sexually inhibited. Many suffer from deep psychological blocks. Many are married to clumsy, inexpert or selfish men. Any of these situations can produce a resistance to intercourse which earns the 'frigid' label and it is commonplace to receive letters from women saying 'My husband says I am frigid', or from men who say that their frigid wives are driving them to look elsewhere for sex.

Q. Before we were married my wife made all kinds of excuses for not making love. I thought she was frightened and that once we were married (a year ago) and her rather strict parents weren't breathing down our necks, all would be well. But she is completely frigid. She refuses to let me have sex unless I threaten to leave or to find someone else. Then she just lies there telling me to hurry and get it over with.

She says I am sex mad. She won't discuss it further than that.

I suggested she should get help, but she says I am the one that needs help because I'm like an animal. But I have had other girl friends and they've never complained.

I love my wife, but I cannot live like this for long.

A. Patience is the number one requirement for you if you want to save your marriage. The kind of threats you have been making are bound to exacerbate the problem.

There could be all sorts of reasons for what you call your wife's frigidity. I refuse to call it that, preferring the word reluctance. Her resistance could be due to your lack of skill, for although you mention previous experiences, these do not necessarily add up to expertise.

One slight clue to your wife's difficulty is your mention of her strict parents. She may have been conditioned to regard sex as sinful or a duty.

You are right, of course, to suggest that she needs help but since she believes that you are the one in need of it, a practical suggestion would be for you both to seek help, preferably from the National Marriage Guidance Council or from a sex therapy clinic if you are lucky enough to have a sympathetic and well-informed doctor.

Offering to share the problem with your wife rather than expecting her to take steps alone to improve matters will make it a lot easier to get her to agree.

You mustn't, at this stage, force her to have intercourse. Show as much affection as you can. Be tender and loving without making demands.

It isn't going to be easy and you may never succeed but unless you try, your marriage seems bound to fail.

The letters I have used here to illustrate some of the problems to do with married sex have merely skimmed the surface. As marriage becomes more complex so do the sexual problems which confront people. Available help is very limited; sex manuals, while useful to some people – if only to stimulate the imagination – are often almost too functional and objective to be satisfactory. As one couple I helped put it, 'We tried a sex manual before writing to you, but it was all rather beyond us and we felt, at the end of it, like a couple of guinea pigs instead of rather worried people who needed a bit of straightforward, commonsense advice.'

Growing Pains

Looking at today's sophisticated young people you'd be tempted to think they knew all the answers. But appearances are misleading. They have the same doubts, fears and hang-ups their parents had, plus the additional problems which today's more complex society bring.

Today's adolescents have grown up in a liberal, materialistic culture. Their expectations are higher than those of their parents at the same age and the need to keep up with the teenage Joneses is more pressing then ever. They must conform – or they feel inferior. Torrid sex, trendy clothes, freedom from controls – both at home and at school – are the objectives for which most of them strive and if they do not achieve them, they blame their spots, their lack of breasts or chests, their parents or lack of cash. The incidence of teenage pregnancies continues to rise alarmingly. Every year, the statistics on schoolgirl abortions show an increase and VD is now second only to measles as the most infectious disease.

These are the most disturbing symptoms of a society in which young people assert their independence of parental and school control more than ever before.

Because rules of behaviour and the sort of firm guide-lines their parents knew have all but vanished, today's children have to make their own rules and decisions but despite their apparent maturity, they are not equipped to cope. Secretly many wish there *were* rules to which they could conform and this is clearly demonstrated in the letters they write, particularly about sex.

But parents who try to lay down laws are up against the 'My friends stay out all night – why can't I?' blackmail, so that it takes a very determined parent these days to impose strict disciplines and those who do, often end up with resentful children on their hands.

It is a contradictory state of affairs. On the one hand, children would appreciate firm parental guidance; on the other, they protest violently against it for the sake of keeping up appearances.

Illustrating this double-think is the situation where a teenager gives a party at home. She announces that she hopes her parents won't stick around to spoil the fun, but just the same, she's secretly relieved if they remain in the house but out of the way so that if the going gets rough and the boys start putting on the sexual pressures, she can say 'Watch it. My boring mother and father are upstairs . . .' without giving away the fact that she's anxious and worried about sexual participation.

But all too often, parents take their nagging children at their word and get out of the house for the sake of a quiet life. Result: more letters from pregnant girls, more letters from young teenagers convinced they've got VD symptoms, more letters from distracted parents who say 'Where did we go wrong?'

The lack of communication between parents and children is the basis of many of the problems with which I am confronted. Girls, particularly, find it difficult if not impossible to talk to their mothers and the silence between mothers and daughters often builds up into deep hostility. To many girls – and boys – I am a surrogate mother.

There's so much confusion and hypocrisy surrounding our moral standards. Teenagers, lectured on all sides about virginity, self-control and decent standards of behaviour, see all around them sharp evidence of the permissive behaviour of their elders. The hypocrisy of it all baffles them. Why should a sixteen-year-old boy abstain from sex when he suspects his father is having an affair? Why should a fifteen-year-old girl say NO to an importunate boy in the parlour when her mother is in bed upstairs with her lover?

Rare and far-fetched illustrations? Not at all. They are shocking but commonplace situations demonstrated daily in letters adolescents send me.

Because the main motivation of the huge majority of

teenagers aged twelve and upwards is the need to be attractive and desirable to the opposite sex, many are obsessed by their appearance and physical development. If a girl hasn't started menstruating by the time she is thirteen, she begins to worry about her sexual development, comparing it to those of her friends who began at eleven or twelve. If her breasts are slow in growing, she is afraid she will be passed by in the highly competitive dating game. Weight is also a serious obsession and countless girls ask for diets and slimming aids.

Boys are equally anxious. They actually send me penis measurements, flaccid and erect, hoping for reassurance that their size is comparably up to standard. They worry, too, if their chests are narrow or if hair on their faces and bodies is slow to appear. But far and away the most dominant anxiety among boys is what they believe to be the dangers of masturbation. Ignorance about this practice brings more guilt and depression and insecurity than any other problem which boys – and some girls – face.

The astonishing myths still abound: 'Will hair grow on the palms of my hands?' 'Will the habit damage my penis?' 'Will I ever be able to have normal sex if I don't stop doing it?' 'Will it make me impotent?' 'Will it stop me having babies?' 'Will it give me heart disease?' 'Is it, as my mother says it is, a sin against God?'

Masturbation is seen as an evil for which due guilt must be endured and often young people count the days of abstinence, like giving up smoking.

Parents are largely to blame for the deep misery and fear from which their masturbating children suffer, for mothers still smack toddlers found doing it, tell them it's a filthy habit, and perpetuate the myths. And fathers, their sons have reported to me, have actually taken the belt to masturbating offspring.

There's a positive catalogue of defects which teenagers write about. A 5′ 7″ sixteen-year-old girl asked if it was possible to have an operation to shorten her legs. Short boys ache to be tall, thin ones to be muscular. Slender girls yearn to increase their measurements, plump ones to reduce them. Blondes want to be brunettes. ('My mother says I am too young to dye my hair. I am eleven. What do you think?') Redheads want to be anything but red.

Common to both sexes is acne, which causes the deepest embarrassment and, in some cases, a worrying neurosis. They do not believe they will ever grow out of it and beg for magic cures.

All their terrors and anxieties are based on their need to be desired and loved and noticed, by their need to make and maintain relationships.

Q. Though I have been out with boys quite often, I never seem to keep one. After one or two dates they're not interested. I know it's my fault and I think there must be something wrong with me.

As soon as a boy starts to kiss or touch me I just go rigid. I can't respond and all I want to do is run away. I am fifteen and most of my friends sleep with their boy friends.

I really would like a steady boy friend but the thought of his expecting to make love just terrifies me. Can you help please?

A. I don't think there is anything wrong with you. You are just a rather old-fashioned girl who knows instinctively that sex with a stranger isn't going to be satisfactory for you.

Not all girls fling virtue gaily aside at the first invitation from a boy despite your girl friends' claims of sexual experience. You don't have to believe all *they* tell you.

I am sure their imagination often runs riot, and very much doubt if they are as experienced as they suggest.

You can't really blame boys for trying it on, for sometimes they are lucky enough to find girls who respond immediately and enthusiastically to the first kiss and are ready to go all the way, just for kicks or under the usually mistaken notion that if they agree to have sex, the boy will remain theirs forever.

There is plenty of time for you to meet a boy who will like you and want to go steady, even though you refuse to fall gasping into his arms after a couple of dates. In fact, I believe you stand a better chance of a permanent and good relationship than those boastful friends of yours.

And when you do meet a boy you can love and respect and who feels the same way about you, the inhibitions and terrors which worry you now will, I am sure, vanish.

*

Q. I am sixteen and my two girl friends and I and our boy friends all go around together. We have decided to go away for a weekend to a cottage owned by one of the girls' parents. My parents aren't very broadminded so I will have to tell them a few white lies.

But that's not my real problem. The other two girls have already slept with their boys, I'm the odd one out. I shall certainly be expected to if we go away, but I'm scared stiff of intercourse and of the possible consequences. I just don't know what to do as I don't want to lose my friends and look foolish. Can you advise me?

A. Yes, I can advise you and I hope you'll take my advice, which is to drop out of this weekend jaunt. If you go, you'll probably find that the pairing-off arrangements will make it impossible for you to avoid sharing a bed with your boy friend. Which means that intercourse is inevitable. You're unlikely to sit up all night together having intellectual discussions. The best way to resist sex is to keep away from tempting situations – tempting to both you and to the boy.

Make some excuse to your friends – a family get-together you can't dodge would do. I cannot believe such close buddies would end your friendship just because you can't participate in the weekend plan. They'd hardly be worth bothering about if they made a big issue out of that.

You're concerned about looking foolish in their eyes. It's much more important to stick to your principles and con-tinue to avoid sex until you're good and ready for it. If you do it just to go along with the rest of the crowd, you'll not only probably hate it and yourself and maybe even your boy

friend, but you could certainly face the possible consequences you so rightly fear.

Teenage love frequently manifests itself in crushes and infatua-
tions for people beyond their reach.

Teenage girls fall wildly in love with pop stars, with television
actors and disc jockeys and often with their teachers or with
older men who are unattainable. Such love, despite the generally
held view that it's unhealthy and should be discouraged is, in
fact, considered by some psychiatrists to be not only harmless
but even therapeutic, provided the infatuation dies the normal
death it almost always does. It's far better for a girl to act out her
passionate fantasies on an untouchable disc jockey than run the
risk of becoming a casualty as a result of an immature relationship with an attainable partner.

Male teachers have a particularly hard time with nubile,
early-maturing girls, convinced they are in love with the man at
the blackboard, and many teachers faced with this problem write
to me.

Q. I know that many male teachers have teenage girl students
who shower them with embarrassing attentions. I face a
similar situation.

After a fairly long spell at a boys' school, I joined a mixed
school a few months ago and I dread each waking day. The
girls make outrageous remarks, send me hair-raising love
letters and get me very hot under the collar.

My wife, amused by it all, says I should ignore them, but
she doesn't have to face them. Any ideas for dealing with
them would be appreciated, please.

A. Although your wife's advice is sound, it isn't, as you say,
easy to follow. You cannot really ignore a bunch of excitable
girls, determined to gain your favours. And the more you
appear to ignore them, the more likely they are to try to break
down your resistance, which is a challenge to them.

I think you must accept their attentions with amiable
equanimity and treat them with good-humoured affection. If

you ever let them realise their behaviour embarrasses you, they'll get you even hotter under the collar in the future.

I dare say every young male teacher in the country has to put up with teenage crushes. Simply accept it all as part of the job. You are at least fortunate that it is a group situation. It's much trickier for a man when one highly developed young female in the class makes a determined effort to get at the teacher. Often she will plot to catch him when he is alone. He can be compromised or even blackmailed and I advise any teacher threatened by this situation to make sure he is always accompanied by a colleague or in the company of other pupils if he feels he is at risk.

I am afraid that some teachers, flattered by the attentions of sexy young girls, are vain enough actually to encourage their attentions. I do not always place the blame for these uncomfortable classroom antics squarely on the shoulders of pupils. Some teachers may be unaware of the effect they have on adolescent girls. Clearly you are all too aware of the possible consequences of schoolgirl infatuation.

Your wife's advice is sound. Take it.

Some girls who fall in love with older men seek a father-figure or a father-substitute and the advice columnist to whom a girl reveals her tortured feelings has to be honest, while trying not to add to the pain of the almost inevitable rejection.

Q. My father died three years ago and since then his business partner has been very good to my mother and me. Over the last six months I've realised that I'm in love with him and I want to be with him all the time. Despite the difference in our age (he is forty-six and I am seventeen), I somehow knew he felt the same for me, so a month ago I told him I loved him. He admitted I was attractive but said my mother would be very upset if she knew how I felt. Since then he hasn't been to see us, although he has taken my mother to lunch twice.

I am desperately unhappy. How can I make him come back and realise that it doesn't matter about our ages or what others think?

A. A big difference in age doesn't matter at all if the two people concerned are deeply in love. As for other people's opinions, well those can be faced up to if a couple are close enough to withstand criticism or condemnation. But I am afraid that in your case, the love is heavily one-sided. You love him (or so you think) but he doesn't love you (or so I think).

When he said you were attractive, I'm pretty certain he said it merely to soften the blow of rejection, though it would have been kinder and more sensible and a lot less cowardly if he'd told you he feels like a father to you. As, I believe, he does. I should think he has stayed away from you because he dreads an emotional scene and can you really blame him? He must feel a lot more comfortable and relaxed with your mother than with her love-lorn daughter.

I don't want to put you down, but I have a strong feeling that you love him because he has taken the place of the father you lost. You love him like a daughter, though you probably won't admit it now. Perhaps it's best for you if he stays away for a time until you get him out of your system. As you will in due course. When he hears you are going around with boys, he'll be right round to take a fatherly interest in your future.

Many of the sexual problems people face in adult life spring from traumatic experiences in childhood or early adolescence and a considerable proportion of letters I receive from very young people describe their shock at some revelation of sexuality between their parents.

Adolescents with whom I have had discussions on the subject find it painful, shocking or just plain unbelievable that parents actually make love. They simply do not relate the knowledge of sex they have acquired to their own parents.

When I ask them how they think they were conceived, they stare blankly. They do not want to admit that their parents have sex. When, as frequently happens, children and young adolescents come upon their parents in the act of love, the result can be traumatic and damaging. And it is gratifying when children seek advice or simply spill out their confused feelings in a letter,

3

for when a child can unburden herself to an objective adult, there's a reasonable chance that the disquieting feelings can be sensibly channelled.

Q. I am fourteen years old and feel very unhappy because by accident I walked into my parents' bedroom the other morning while they were making love. It was terribly embarrassing and now I feel very uncomfortable and unnatural with them and they are acting strangely towards me. None of us has said anything and I wonder if I should say something to my mother. The atmosphere at home now is awful. I thought what they were doing was horrible. Can you tell me what I should do?

A. Poor you. It was a very unfortunate thing to happen to you – discovering your parents in the sex act.

I imagine you know a bit about what happens when people make love, but it can be pretty shocking when you see it happening between your parents and realise it's all real and not just talk.

I am afraid that sometimes when children accidentally see their parents making love, it puts them off sex and I hope this won't happen to you. I don't think it will, for you sound very sensible and nice.

It's naturally difficult for children to accept the fact that they wouldn't have been born at all if their parents hadn't made love. Most children cannot associate their parents with sex, perhaps because many children have the idea that it's kind of nasty and secretive and even dirty. I am sure you know that's not true.

There's another reason why some teenagers think sex between older people is disgusting: they think it's something only young people do, which is rubbish, of course. Many, many people much older than your parents find happiness and fulfilment in love-making as you will one day discover for yourself.

I think the best thing you can do to improve the atmosphere at home is say to your mother you are sorry you burst in on them the other day and you reckon they must have felt as rotten about it as you did. I dare say your mother would like to pluck up courage to talk to you first, but I expect she's even more embarrassed than you are and it would be a great kindness on your part to relieve her mind.

As for your feelings towards your parents – be glad they are happy and that they love one another. I bet a lot of your less fortunate friends have parents who fight like dogs and never know the contentment and happiness your parents share – and which is all part of a truly loving and full family life.

*

Q. Almost every night I lie in bed waiting to hear my mum and dad make love. I've tried to ignore it but I just can't. I always know because their bed squeaks so loudly.

It's not very nice for a thirteen-year-old girl to tell a stranger all about your own parents' sexual habits, but it's getting on my nerves.

What I can't understand is that they often quarrel like mad, so why do they keep on making love? I know it would embarrass them if I said anything but I don't think I can stand much more of it.

A. The first thing you should do is accept the fact that parents make love to each other. And be pleased that yours do. It proves that in spite of their quarrels, they still like each other enough to be happy and loving in private.

Quarrels between married couples might sound rough and fraught – but they're often merely letting off steam and being perfectly natural and uninhibited in their behaviour towards each other which is great. It's also great that they make love. If they didn't, the hostility they sometimes show could be more serious.

I know it's difficult for children to accept the fact that their parents have sex. It must seem pretty nasty to you. But try to remember that as well as being your parents, they are also a couple of human beings who love and need each other in every way. If the creaking bed springs keep you awake, stuff your ears with cotton wool – and go to sleep congratulating yourself that your parents care about each other. A lot of children would lead much happier lives if their parents were as loving as yours are.

If more parents were aware of the anxieties from which their children secretly suffer, fewer children, perhaps, would need to write to a stranger for comfort and reassurance. Often, as in the following letter, children write in pairs.

Q. We are very worried about our mother. About three months ago, our parents let the spare room to a man. Since then, our mother has changed a lot. She has had her hair done blonde and bought some new clothes and she's stopped slopping around the house in old slacks. In fact, she now looks very sexy. She and this man went out twice to the pub while our father stayed home and watched TV.

We are afraid there might be trouble ahead and wonder if we ought to warn our father, who never bothers about a thing and is very easy-going.

We are sisters, aged thirteen and fourteen. Do you think we should warn our father or talk to our mother?

A. Neither. Just don't let your imagination run away with you. I reckon you've been reading too many lurid stories about ladies having love affairs with lodgers.

I dare say the reason your mother got her hair done up and some new clothes is because the lodger's rent helped the family budget. Knowing how hard it is to bring up a family these days, I guess she probably scrimped to buy things for you two girls.

As for the visits to the pub – nothing wrong there. Your dad, presumably, could have gone too if he'd felt like it. Maybe he prefers TV to beer at the bar. But you can bet your sweet lives that easy-going as your father is, he's unlikely to be so short-sighted as not to suspect any fishy carry-on, if fishy carry-on there is.

Naturally, if your mother went out every single night with the lodger, there might be cause for alarm and need for a reminder to your father that mother ought to have a break now and then. It is true that husbands can get lazy and complacent. They are also apt to be unimaginative and some are too downright selfish to bother about whether their wives are happy or not.

Your mother is lucky to have daughters so concerned about her – but don't look for trouble that exists only in the mind. Just be glad that the presence of another man around the house bucked her up a bit.

When I sent that reply off to those two worried little girls, I will confess to some dishonesty – some bending of the truth. I wanted to reassure them but I feared that they were right in their assessment of their mother's relationship with the other man.

I published their letter in the *Daily Mirror* in the hope that the parents would see my reply and identify themselves with the situation, although, as is my practice, I changed some of the details so that the family couldn't be precisely identified. Sometimes, in order to maintain the confidentiality which is so important, I change ages or even the sex of the writers. For instance, the two children in this case could have been boys or brother and sister. And the mother might have been originally a greying mouse who dyed her hair bright yellow to attract the other man.

Children often write letters which underline their insecurity in family situations, especially in one-parent families. I have found that an understanding approach, coupled with straight talk, helps children to put adult relationships into perspective.

Q. My brother is thirteen and I am nearly fifteen. Our father died eight years ago and since then we've all been really happy together. But lately our mother has been going out with a man. He even comes to stay at weekends, and we suspect he sleeps in her room. She can't do enough for him and tells us how nice and kind he is.

Neither my brother nor I like him and we couldn't stand having him around all the time. Do you think we should tell her before she gets to like him too much?

A. I see jealousy rearing its ugly head here. Your poor mother must be desperate, knowing you two are spying on her and resenting her friendship with this man. I don't suppose it has ever occurred to either of you – and there's no reason why, at your age, it should have – that she misses male companionship. She loves you both – but she can love someone else too without harming you or depriving you of her affection.

One of these days you are going to fall in love and you'll go off and leave your mother without a qualm – as you should. But when that happens she'll be very lonely. You ought to be glad there will be someone around to comfort her and look after her.

You say you don't like this man. Maybe that's because you don't like the *idea* of him and haven't even bothered to find out if he's as nice as your mother says he is. He must be – otherwise she wouldn't care for him.

Stop being selfish – and stop prying. What are you doing, anyway, snooping around in the night to find out where he's sleeping? Stop being a couple of Peeping Toms and be thankful if your mother has now got the man around the house she needs and deserves.

Although the majority of letters about their regular and frequent habit of masturbating come from worried boys, many girls endure the torture of guilt and misery. . . .

Q. I am a seventeen-year-old girl, in desperate need of advice. I cannot discuss my problem with anyone for people would think me disgusting.

Ever since I was quite young, I have had a physical sex habit from which I get great satisfaction but feel awful afterwards. Not ill, just very miserable and depressed. I am also worried because I have an idea that girls who do this cannot have a proper sex life later and I believe it makes women frigid and they may not be able to have children.

Can you tell me if I am abnormal and what to do about it?

A. Not to mince words, what you engage in is masturbation, of which there are several forms and methods. Let me put you right on a few facts.

Masturbation, whether it is practised by girls or boys, does not make the slightest difference to their subsequent ability to enjoy 'normal' sexual relationships with the opposite sex. It is not disgusting. It does not make boys impotent or girls frigid nor does it prevent people having babies.

What *could* have an effect on your future relationships is your mental attitude to this habit. You could repress normal feelings because of the guilt masturbating gives you.

There is no reason whatsoever for feeling miserable or depressed. Actually, you feel depressed because you believe, quite falsely, that what you do is morally wrong. It is guilt which brings on the miserable aftermath – and it is quite unnecessary guilt.

In time you will meet the right boy and be able to enjoy the pleasures of shared sex within a loving relationship. But until then, there's no reason, either medical or moral, why you should not obtain private release for your pent-up feelings.

With the alarmingly high incidence of schoolgirl and teenage pregnancy, it is not surprising that a very large proportion of my letters are from pregnant girls, lonely in their desperation, begging for help. How, they ask, can they get abortions? Who should they go to? Most are terrified to see a doctor, particularly their family doctor, for they are convinced that he will inform their parents.

Advising a fourteen or fifteen-year-old girl about abortion, through a letter, with no opportunity for person-to-person counselling, would of course be dangerous and wrong.

I do my best to try to persuade girls to talk to their mothers, for in my experience, after the first shock and horror has subsided, most mothers prefer to help their daughters to get abortions than to allow the pregnancy to continue. Few women would choose to be grandmothers of their children's illegitimate offspring. But many girls, terrified to reveal their secret, leave it too late for a safe termination.

It is astonishing how many girls tell me that they are five or six months pregnant and have managed to conceal the fact from their mothers. Some frightened girls leave home and live rough rather than confess, and this sort of situation is just another demonstration of the lack of communication between parents and their children.

When young girls beg for abortion advice, I refer them to one of several responsible advisory bodies upon whom I feel I can rely. But not every pregnant girl wants a termination. . . .

Q. When my boy friend persuaded me to have sex, he said that if anything happened he'd stand by me and we'd get married. But when I discovered I was two months pregnant and I told him, he said he didn't want to know.

I am terrified to tell my parents and begged my boy friend to come with me to break the news but he flatly refused and I haven't seen him for five weeks.

I am sixteen and a half and now nearly four months pregnant and out of my mind with worry. Is there any way I can force him to marry me? If not, what can I do? My parents still do not know, although I've noticed my mother looking at me rather curiously. Please, please help.

A. The first thing you *must* do is tell your mother. Her curious looks may mean she already half suspects.

I know you're scared, but you can't hide your pregnancy much longer from your mother's keen eyes, and the sooner you can bring yourself to tell her, the sooner you'll be able to get help. For although she'll be upset, of course, I am sure that once she's got over the shock, she'll do everything she can for you and your baby.

As for the boy, there's no way you can force him to marry you. And it would be a very big mistake to try. You've got to face the sad fact that he doesn't love you and, awful as it is, I'm afraid you'll have to cope without him.

I dare say you're thinking how unfair life is to girls. Boys can simply walk away, leaving girls with all the worry and the responsibility of their babies. But that's the way it is and that's why your mother is the best person possible for you to share your worries with. She'll help you to decide whether to keep the baby or arrange for it to be adopted. She'll help with the practical arrangements for the birth – after all, she knows all about having babies.

If you decide to keep the baby, your mother and father may feel that the boy ought, at least, to pay towards its maintenance. They'll need to seek a solicitor's advice about how to make a claim against him.

I am very sorry for you, for I know how lonely you must be feeling. But you'll be a lot less lonely once you've found the courage to speak up at home.

Often, at the end of a long day of reading problem letters, I go home sad and depressed and frustrated. But every now and then I become enraged and my determination to be coolly objective and sympathetic no matter what, wavers.

Q. The girl I have been going out with is five months pregnant and both our parents are pressuring us to marry.

I should have taken more care but she was more than willing and I don't see why I should be the one to pay for the mistake.

My girl friend says she would marry for the sake of the baby – but reluctantly. We don't love each other and we know it wouldn't work. We would have to live with her parents whom I can't stand and who have no time for me.

As she is only eighteen and I am nineteen, I honestly feel the baby would be better off being adopted – don't you agree?

3*

A. I do, indeed, agree. If ever a couple were unfit for and unsuited for parenthood, it is you and your girl friend.

I'd feel very sorry indeed for a baby being reared by such an irresponsible pair, though I'm glad to note you realise you should have been more careful.

To marry in all the circumstances would be madness. There would be very little hope that you'd stay together and you might well bring more unwanted children into the world.

If the expected baby is adopted, you can be sure – if you are interested in its welfare – that it will certainly be wanted and brought up by parents who yearn to have a child to love.

Don't give in to parents' pressure to wed, for despite their understandable desire to have a grandchild, if you marry that child will be the victim of several selfish citizens more concerned with their own self-interest than the interest of the innocent infant.

Sorry, but I can't resist a passing comment. Your girl-friend's parents, you say, have no time for you. I haven't much, either. For you or for your irresponsible girl.

The Affair

Almost every wife who writes to tell me that her marriage is in ruins puts the blame squarely on the other woman – the woman, she says, who has 'stolen' her husband.

I take the view that seldom can another woman be entirely blamed for the split; she just happens to be on the scene when the marriage is shaky. Or the restless or unhappy husband searches for her when the matrimonial going gets rough.

Some wives have the misfortune to marry dedicated women-chasers, immature men unable to maintain a steady relationship with any woman including those they marry and those they use for temporary sex or excitement. Rarely do such men manage to achieve the maturity required to make marriage work. Women who marry them are sad casualties with little hope and I often advise them to cut their losses if it's possible in practical terms.

The more commonplace situation is that of a man married, usually, for several years, who meets or finds another woman whom he may see as a replacement for his wife. Or, not wanting to tear up domestic roots, keeps under wraps as his secret mistress. Until his wife finds out.

An interesting survey into the association of married men and their mistresses revealed that only one in ten of the unfaithful husbands interviewed actually married the women with whom they had affairs, indicating that despite their high hopes of taking over the wife's role, women who have affairs with married men are unlikely to achieve that happy ending. When it comes to the moment of decision, the majority of men – if the survey I have mentioned presents an accurate assessment – drop their mistresses, preferring an uneasy marriage to the upheaval of separation.

Many men have told me that an affair is fine, so long as it doesn't interfere with married life. They enjoy the sex, the admiration and the exciting knife-edge fear of discovery which alleviates some of the boredom of domesticity. But divorce, with its legal wrangles over children and property, its threat to peace of mind, to financial stability, possibly to a career, becomes unthinkable.

Even at the trivial level of a wife's expertise in ironing his shirts and running his home, a man can hesitate about moving in with a woman who might be very good in bed but whose domestic skills are limited to pouring hot water on a tea bag and defrosting a TV supper.

The wife who writes bitterly about the other woman may be distraught, humiliated and deeply hurt, but the other women – the mistresses who tell me their stories – certainly do not appear to enjoy the bliss they expected when they began an affair with another woman's husband. They are the girls who live on intermittent sex and the never-ending hope that one day in the vague rosy future, their lover will finally make up his mind and leave his wife and the months and years of waiting will turn out to have been worthwhile.

It is this hope which keeps the other woman going, which makes it possible for her to live out her shadowy existence in the background of her lover's life. It is hope which makes it possible for her to wait for the phone to ring, or accept, philosophically, the times when it remains silent. It's the hope of a final happy ending which compensates for the loneliness, for lost friends abandoned because *he* just might turn up unexpectedly when his mistress has made a date with a friend. Friends must be sacrificed on the altar of part-time love.

The girl who elects to be the other woman in a man's life learns very early on in the relationship what sacrifice means. They are sacrifices the wife never has to make.

'You know I want to celebrate my birthday with you, darling,' he says, 'but *she's* fixed up this party and got champagne in and the children are looking forward to it and I can't let them down. We'll have our private celebration when I can snatch an hour or two and I promise you it'll be an unforgettable celebration. . . .'

'I'll only be away a fortnight, sweetheart,' he says, 'it'll go in a flash. I've got to take them away for a holiday. She'd get very suspicious if I tried to get out of it now. I'll try to send you a postcard but you're not to worry if you don't hear from me. You'll know I will be thinking of you every minute of the day – and especially at night. . . .'

'I did try to stop her arranging for us to go to dinner with the Joneses on Friday,' he says, 'I know it's our special night but she's got the babysitter laid on and I can't do a thing about it. You can have a nice early night and some of those special dreams. . . .'

The girl who chooses to be the other woman soon discovers what jealousy means. She lies awake at night, torturing herself with her images of his happy family life. Is he making love to his wife? Does he, in spite of his protestations to the contrary, enjoy it?

Should she maintain a grain of independence and go out with another man occasionally, even though she dreads the jealous scenes he'll make? Of course she's glad he's so possessive but maybe a night out now and then would show him other men are interested too. It might even get him nearer to making the big decision to leave the wife who has first claim.

The girl who agrees to become the other woman rapidly acquires the art of being furtive. Like making 'coded' phone calls to his office and meeting him in out of the way restaurants and pubs where he's not known. Like sitting in the car parked in some dark back street and checking carefully in case she's left her lipstick or her lighter before he drives off home.

She soon learns how to co-operate in his furtive activities. She is careful not to buy him gifts he will have to explain. She avoids wearing strong perfume his wife could identify as not being hers. She is prepared to drop everything to meet him at a moment's notice. She steels herself to pretend mere casual friendship if she and her lover meet in public.

One of the hardest disciplines the other woman has to

practise is never being able to talk about her lover or show him off to her family and friends. And, as any woman who chooses this role will confirm, it is often the trivial little things which are the hardest to take. Like never being the one to care for him when he's ill and never even being able to sew a loose button on his overcoat in case his wife asks him who repaired it. For his wife is the one who enjoys these simple rights – not his girl friend.

So why *do* women settle for what seems like such hellish second best?

Love, they say, is the only reason. But I believe there are other reasons, too. There is the attraction of the unattainable, the satisfaction of secretly owning a man who legally belongs to someone else, the triumph of one woman who gains another woman's possession. There is the sexual excitement, maintained at a high pitch, never sinking to the mundane routine of married sex. There is the romance and mystery which surround the secrecy of illicit love.

There is the plus side to the uncertainty, living with the prospect of the next snatched, passionate fulfilment. There is the certain knowledge of being wanted and needed. And the glowing reward of the sacrifices made for his happiness – the sacrifice of returning him to the wife and family whose needs, he claims, are so much greater than those of his mistress.

But most of the girls who are the third corner of a matrimonial triangle reach a point of desperation. Should they try to leave him? Should they issue an ultimatum? Typical of countless letters from the unhappy other woman are these two. . . .

Q. Please help a part-time 'wife'. From Monday to Thursday, the man I love lives with me in London, where his business is. Every Friday evening, he drives two hundred miles to his legal wife and their two children. This fantastic situation has been going on for more than five years and I have reached the stage when I am so unhappy, I don't know what to do.

He spends his holidays with her and the children out of duty, he says. He swears he loves only me and that we'd marry if he was free but he won't leave her while the children are young. He says he is fond of his wife and will do nothing to hurt her. Yet he constantly hurts me. I, too, want children by him.

I am kept out of sight in case we're even seen together. My weekends are long and lonely.

I am now twenty-nine and so far as I can see, might be forty-nine before I become a real full-time wife. Do you think I'd be wise to issue an ultimatum to him? I am terrified to do anything that might cause us to break up.

A. What staggers me is how your lover has managed to keep you under wraps for so long. How he's been able to deceive his wife for five years. He is a clever man. Clever enough to have persuaded you to live like a hermit for the sake of your nights of unwedded bliss. Clever enough to enjoy the best of all worlds. But you're not very clever at all. You are no match for your lover.

He knows you will endure this situation because you love him. I suppose you do love him or you certainly wouldn't submit to being a prisoner.

Are you sure it isn't only sex that keeps you so enslaved? Are you, perhaps, afraid that at twenty-nine you won't ever find another man? One thing I'm pretty sure of : if you issue that ultimatum, you'll lose him. I think he'll still stay married to his unsuspecting wife. He'd simply find another accommodating girl friend. He's certainly clever enough for that.

It seems to me you are the loser all round. I doubt if you've got the courage or strength of will to tell him he must choose between you and his wife. If you were sure of him, you wouldn't have written to me.

I'd like to advise you to cut yourself free of him but I don't think you'd take the slightest notice, more's the pity. At forty-nine, you just may be his wife. But I doubt it.

*

Q. When I met the man I am in love with, I did not know he was married. He was evasive and never actually said he was free but let me assume it. We had been going together for six months when I became pregnant and it wasn't until I pressed him to marry me that he confessed he had a wife and two children. You can imagine my despair.

He said he would leave her and set up home with me, but two years have now gone by and nothing has changed. He says he loves me but that his legitimate children have first claim. He comes to see me when he can. I go to work and leave my daughter with a baby-minder and it's an awful life.

I want to believe him when he assures me we'll have a full life together when his other children are old enough but I am so depressed and feel so hopeless that although I am only twenty-five, life doesn't seem worth living. What hope have I, do you think, that he will keep his promise?

A. Very little, I fear. I have heard this story so often – the one about waiting until the children are old enough to stand on their own feet, and all the other fine excuses men make. Have you ever asked him the age he reckons that his children will need to reach before he can abandon them? Is it when they are sixteen or eighteen? Or when they get married? You will have a long, long wait, I'm afraid. You might have to wait forever. I can believe you when you say you have an awful life and I think it will go on being awful and will, in fact, get worse, unless you take a firm grip of the situation you are in and make some changes.

Change number one should be to bid your lover farewell. You love him, you say, so it is going to be very very hard to be firm but for your own and your daughter's sake you ought to try. Otherwise you are going to spend the rest of your life waiting for his visits, which, I assume, mean a quick leap into bed before he goes back home to his wife.

Your child will never know what it's like to have a real father. You will never have more than a part-time lover. And if his wife finds out about you, you can be sure you won't see him even occasionally.

Change number two should be to try to find some new friends. Look for a babysitter and try to get out now and then. Maybe one night out a week at evening classes would give you a chance to widen your interests and meet people with similar ones. You are too young to give up hope of finding a better way of living and tough as it will be to do it, I hope you will take my advice and give this man up while time is still on your side.

A considerable – and increasing – proportion of letters concerning the third corner of the marriage triangle comes from men whose wives have taken lovers and the fact that more and more women leave their husbands and children for another man is another symptom of women's newfound independence. When I first became an advice columnist, it was comparatively rare for women to leave the matrimonial home to move in with a lover, especially if she had children but more and more women now are prepared to abandon their children.

When the Finer Report on One-Parent Families was taking evidence (I was a member of the Finer Committee which prepared the government report) we found that about one-third of all lone parents were men. Some, of course, are widowers; some are married to women who left because the marriage became unendurable. But many are men whose wives have found lovers and the pathetic letters they send indicate their bewilderment and their inability to cope with the domestic role which most women take so easily in their stride.

Many deserted husbands give up their jobs and live on social security benefits in order to be both mother and father to their children. Some seek 'housekeepers' who will, they hope, fulfil not only the domestic role but will also be accommodating in bed.

Curiously, men are apt to be more understanding about the reasons why their wives left them. They say 'I realise now that she had a terrible struggle with money. . . .' 'I neglected her and the children. . . .' 'I took her for granted. . . .' 'I never took her out and she obviously became bored. . . .' 'I never listened to her when she wanted to discuss our problems. . . .' More men, in my experience, are ready to take back erring wives than women are to forgive straying husbands.

Often the cynical thought creeps into my mind, as I'm reading a letter from a remorseful man, that his eagerness for her return could have something to do with the cost of replacing a wife with hired help. It's a nasty thought which I try to banish, though sometimes the urge to say 'It serves you right' to the sort of man who writes 'If only I could have my time over again' is almost irresistible.

Regrettably, many men write to me about their wives' departure too late for any advice which might have prevented the parting and all I can do then is offer comfort and hope that she'll return. But when a husband's suspicion is aroused, there is sometimes a chance that a marriage threatened by a wife's affair already begun or contemplated can be saved. . . .

Q. For some months I have suspected that my wife has a lover. We have been happily married for fifteen years although during the past year or so, she has been restless and has seemed bored. She has never worked since our marriage and our only child is away at school.

Of course, I have never actually seen my wife and this man making love, but I suspect he goes to the house during the day while I am at work. Naturally, I am upset and worried. I want to save my marriage. I do not know whether to tell her I am aware of what is going on – or ignore it in the hopes that it will pass.

A. You would, in my view, be foolish to confront your wife with an accusation of infidelity. It might bring matters to a head and result in the very thing you are so desperate to avoid: the breakdown of your marriage. Difficult as it is for you to live with the knowledge that she may be sleeping with another man, I advise you to try to conceal it for a while longer.

You seem very sure she's cheating but could you be mistaken? Opportunity doesn't always add up to adultery and it may be she is simply seeking companionship to alleviate her boredom. It's a pity she is so bored for there's so much a woman can do – apart from making adulterous love in the afternoons – to find interesting outlets.

Your best move, I think, would be to drop little hints indicating you have your suspicions. If she thinks you are on the alert, she may be scared into dropping this man. Your natural instinct must be to demand an explanation for his visits – but I don't think it's a sensible course to take. You stand a better chance of saving your marriage by playing a patient, watchful game, though it's a very difficult game to play. I hope you will win it.

*

Q. For five years we were happy enough until ten months ago, when my wife started having an affair with a divorced man. When I discovered it, she promised to stop seeing him. But she hasn't stopped and none of my threats to leave her have been any use. She says she doesn't at the moment want to live with him, but they openly flaunt their relationship. I feel I must try to preserve my marriage for the sake of our two young children. If it wasn't for me doing most of the house-work and cooking they would have a very bad time. I don't suppose you have any practical advice to give me, for there seems to be no solution.

A. I think you have acted very weakly. You are letting your wife get away with murder. Literally. She is killing your marriage and destroying the stable life of your children. She is a greedy woman, determined to have her cake and eat it, no matter who else goes hungry.

It's no use making idle threats for she knows perfectly well you don't intend to carry them out. She knows you are a doormat, that you'll make feeble protests while you carry on doing more than your fair share at home to keep the family intact.

If her affair is a temporary infatuation with a man who provides her with brief sexual excitement, I'd say be patient in the hope that she'll get over it and come to her senses. It's

odd that she doesn't appear to want a permanent relationship with this man. Perhaps the truth is that he doesn't want
one with her. If I sound hard on her it's because as I see it,
she's treating you very badly. You may deserve it. You might
have been an inconsiderate and selfish husband. I don't
know, hearing only your side of the story. But if you are
satisfied that you've done everything a husband could do to
make his wife happy and keep her faithful and contented,
then I strongly advise you to put your vague threats into
action – the sort of action which might make her realise
what she's losing if she doesn't face up to the reality of
marriage and motherhood.

If you prove to her that you are strong and determined, her
respect and love could well be re-awakened and you'd have a
good chance to rebuild your marriage on a more solid
foundation.

Although it's generally women who write about the misery of
being the other woman in a married man's life, every now and
again, a despairing letter comes from the other man in a
married woman's life. . . .

Q. I am a bachelor aged thirty. Some months ago, I fell in love
with a beautiful woman. It wasn't until some time after we'd
met that she told me she was married, with two small
children. She says she didn't tell me at first because she didn't
want to lose me. She refuses to make a decision about our
future or to commit herself, telling me to wait and to be
patient. She is very concerned about the children, she says.

Her husband knows nothing about us and she is terrified
he'll find out. We make love whenever we can and I am crazy
about her. But the uncertainty about the future drives me
mad. I wonder whether to go and see her husband and bring
the whole affair into the open.

A. I advise you to do no such thing for as likely as not, you'll
get a punch on the nose from him and a passionate denial
from her that you're anything but just good friends. I also

advise you to detach yourself from this lady as swiftly as you can, for I suspect she is merely entertaining herself with you – getting excitement and sex on the side without the intention of making a permanent commitment. She's not the only wife who, a bit bored perhaps with marriage, amuses herself with someone else.

She's terrified, you say, that her husband will find out. She apparently also enjoys the danger which is all part of the excitement.

I am truly sorry you love her, for it seems to me that it is doomed to be an unrequited love. I think that if her husband knew or if she thought he suspected, she'd give you up without a qualm. If she intended to leave her husband for you, I think she'd have made her position clear by now. You could put her to the test by saying you won't see her again until she decides. And carry out your intention. You'll be putting yourself to the test too and discovering if what you feel for her is, indeed, love and not merely sexual attraction for a beautiful, unattainable woman.

Can a broken marriage involving a third party ever be re-cemented? That is a question I am asked over and over again and there is no short answer. It depends upon the extent of the matrimonial 'crime', and on the personality and strength of character of the principles. Some people are charitable and forgiving; others forgive without generosity, never forgetting to wear their haloes.

There are women who positively enjoy the role of saintly martyrdom, others who go in for the stiff upper lip show, making sure the lip can be seen to quiver now and then. Then too there are the brisk forgivers: 'Okay, let's forget it and we won't ever mention it again but just you make certain there's no repeat performance.' And there are those whose heavy sighs and red-rimmed eyes are a constant reproach and reminder to the culprit who must often wish he'd never come home.

Men, as I've said, seem to be more able to forgive and to carry on as before, though it isn't easy to understand why. Perhaps men, on the whole, are less insecure, are more easily able to reassert their dominant masculinity than women are to re-establish their bruised egos.

When reconciliation *does* work well, it's encouraging that people of both sexes sometimes write to say that the affair which almost wrecked the marriage has, in fact, enriched it. Both men and women, in these cases, have been able to take stock, to be analytical about the reasons why the disaster occurred and to endeavour to improve the relationship so that it will never again be necessary to find consolation outside it.

When people write asking what chance they have of restoring a marriage in which infidelity has been one of the symptoms of the breakdown, I warn them of the difficulties which lie ahead. . . .

Q. After nine years of marriage, I left my husband four years ago because of his affair with another woman. He visits my home regularly to see our two children, aged eight and six, and although he still lives with the other woman, he says they are no longer happy. Recently he asked me if I would take him back, but I dread a repeat of the past. The children adore him and I must admit that he is more considerate now than he ever was and he assures me that things would be different this time.

A. Only you know how much reliance you feel you can put on your husband's assurance that history won't repeat itself. One question you must ask yourself is why he went off with someone else. Is he the type of man who needs the excitement of an extra-marital relationship?

You should also take a long hard look at yourself as a wife. Perhaps, when the children came, you devoted yourself more to them than to him, as do so many young mothers. Perhaps you were aloof in bed, submissive rather than a participant. Perhaps you were a shrewish nagger. These questions need to be carefully weighed and answered before you decide that a second try could work.

It is obvious that he loves the children. But unless you can be certain he loves you, too (and that you love him), the second time round could be as hopeless as the first. If he sees you merely as a refuge from his present unsatisfactory life, in no time at all he'll be off again, seeking someone else. I think that unless you can be as certain as is possible in an uncertain world that there is real hope for the future, you would be wise not to risk yet another miserable disappointment and upheaval for yourself and your children.

*

Q. When my wife went away with her sister for a fortnight's holiday, I did a very stupid thing. I took a girl home to our flat and made love to her in our bed. I don't know whether it was my guilty conscience or what which gave my wife a clue, but she guessed what had happened, taxed me about it and although I lied at first, I finally confessed. All hell broke loose. She left but returned home after a few days. Now she hardly speaks to me, will not sleep in our bed, is sleeping on the sofa in the living room. I have begged her to forgive me and have sworn it won't happen again, but I can't get through to her and don't know what to do to try to restore my marriage, which has been a happy one for nearly ten years.

A. It isn't surprising that all hell broke loose when your wife found out that another woman had occupied her bed. Wives are understandably very sensitive indeed in such situations and you can hardly expect her to be ready yet to forgive what she regards as a desecration. It's hard enough, goodness knows, for wives to accept a foolish slip, but they are particularly hurt and outraged when it happens within their own home and in their own bed. It isn't going to be easy for you to convince her that the whole thing was a stupid misdemeanour. But there is one small consolation for you in all this: she did come back home to you. She is still speaking to you – if coldly.

I imagine that she, too, really wants her marriage to go on, otherwise she'd have stayed away. . . . You will have to be patient and hope that, in time, her broken trust can be restored. Your behaviour must be impeccable. You must get home at the expected, usual time and not be tempted to have a drink on the way to help brace yourself for a difficult evening. You must show her every consideration and continue to try to reassure her. You could even offer to buy a new bed.

I think that in time she will want to relent and at the first sign of softening, suggest a weekend away from home when, I hope, you'll have a beautiful reconciliation. It is not likely to happen for a while yet, though. You can expect her to make you suffer before she decides to resume the relationship you so carelessly disregarded when you presented another woman with the hospitality of your matrimonial bed.

When one partner takes a lover, it's not unusual for the other to do likewise in a spirit of 'I'll get even with him – or her.' It would be dangerous to recommend this as a therapeutic treatment for a sick marriage, but if the couple can be reconciled, there is a chance that the marriage will regain health and be stronger than ever it was. . . .

Q. For some time I have been having an affair with a married man. I don't love him, but he is sexually exciting.

I suppose you are wondering why I did it. I married young, ten years ago, and everything had become stale and I was bored. Life with my husband was so predictable. But I've been well and truly paid back, for while I was enjoying myself, my husband had also been having an affair, and has now left me for this other girl.

He began sleeping with her, he said, when he found out I had a lover. Apart from the misery, I am appalled that we've made such a mess of a marriage which started so happily. I don't suppose you can help but where, I wonder, did we go wrong?

A. I'd need to be an oracle if I could tell you where you went wrong and oracle I am not. But I could make a few guesses.

Life was predictable, you say. And boring – and it's

obvious that neither you nor your husband ever realised that a good marriage doesn't just happen by accident. It has to be worked at. It needs constant renewal. It needs sexual imagination. It needs communication. When marriage is allowed to become a dreary habit, the partners are bound to be tempted to put it at risk by casting around elsewhere for the fun that's missing. Instead of discussing the stale condition of your marriage with your equally bored husband, you found escape with another partner. And he took his revenge.

It is, as you say, a very sad situation but perhaps you could profit by your mistakes. Perhaps it's not too late for a salvage operation. Could you arrange a meeting with your husband, suggesting that you need to get together to sort things out between you? Then ask him what you asked me: 'Where did we go wrong?' With luck, he might have a contribution to make. With luck, you could begin again, now both wiser about the reasons for the break-up.

But if your luck's out and a reconciliation is impossible, try to rebuild your life and develop some rewarding interests. Otherwise you'll drift from one sexual encounter to another. There's nothing, in the end, more boring than that.

There is an enormously wide range of problems based on the advent of the other woman – or the other man – in a marriage. Sometimes the wife wins in the end. Less often, the mistress is triumphant. The losers, always, are the children.

The Anguish of Loneliness

Almost every problem with which an advice columnist is confronted is difficult to solve, but none are more daunting than the problems of the lonely. For lonely people are nearly always inhibited people, shy and introspective, unable to make or maintain relationships.

They come in all ages and social classes. The well-off are just as likely to be isolated as are the poor, the young as the old. There are too, of course, some people in special circumstances, whose loneliness is imposed upon them by these circumstances. I am thinking of the young lone mother, deserted or widowed or unmarried, imprisoned in a home from which she cannot escape because she must care for her children.

Many young people are lonely because their inhibitions make it impossible for them to relate to others in their age group, while middle-aged women find that loneliness overtakes them when the children to whom they've devoted their busy lives have left home.

Shy men, unable to make easy friendships with women, plead for help in finding girl friends, while widows and widowers, suddenly bereft of companionship after years of marriage, are back on a shelf of loneliness, longing to make new friendships, but not knowing how to go about it. Divorced women too can be extremely lonely. They describe how the circle of friends once shared as a couple mysteriously melts away when the wife is on her own. It's a lot easier for a divorced man to pick up the threads of single life. He can go alone into pubs and bars, has less trouble, generally, finding a new woman than a woman has in finding a new man.

The books of marriage bureaux and introduction agencies are

overflowing with women; men are at a premium and the chances of a woman over fifty finding a new partner are slender. The trouble, as the agencies keep reminding me, is that the over-fifty men demand women under forty. And very often find them, leaving older ladies to continue their unavailing search.

Loneliness is one of the near-incurable diseases of old age, for both sexes. The most pathetic letters of all come from elderly women, abandoned by their children, living in bed-sitters or old people's homes simply waiting to die but clinging to life in the vain hope that one day a son or daughter will turn up to rescue them, to want them, to love them. Many ask me to appeal to their families on their behalf, to ask a daughter-in-law to relent, for daughters-in-law are seen as the main reason why sons neglect their ageing lonely parents.

The fact is – and it's a fact I couldn't possibly point out to them – that many old ladies are cantankerous and demanding. Wives who have genuinely tried to make their elderly mothers-in-law welcome and happy write despairingly about the disruption to family life, the problems a querulous old person creates in the home, the resultant quarrels among teenage children and with husbands.

'What shall we do with granny?' was the title of a BBC TV documentary in which I took part. At the end of it, we all agreed that there was simply no practical answer to the question. Which is why so many lonely old people write their pitiful letters; at least they have a link with another human being, even if it's with a stranger.

In many cases, I have been able to make arrangements for welfare workers to call on lonely old people, either too proud or too timid to seek help. But it's impossible for the over-stretched, undermanned social services departments to keep track of all the old people living in isolation. When the lone elderly write to me, I can mount a rescue operation. But for the comparatively few who write, there are countless distressed old people eating out their hearts in loneliness.

Typical of such letters in this one . . .

Q. I have lived on my own for twelve years, since my dear husband died and at the age of seventy-six, I am finding it increasingly difficult to manage my tiny flat. My only son lives some distance away and rarely visits me. I do not get on with my daughter-in-law who has never had much time for me.

I am very lonely, for neighbours don't want to know either. More and more, I wonder if it's worth struggling on alone, for life has no point for people like me.

There is no ideal solution to this kind of problem, no hope I can offer of a family reunion, no way of alerting indifferent neighbours to this woman's plight.

I wrote to her, of course, trying to comfort her, to assure her that there *are* people who care, and I asked her if she would like someone to visit her. I enquired about local facilities for the elderly in her area and told her what they were and when she wrote again to say she'd be very glad of a visitor, I arranged for a welfare worker to call.

I would very much have liked to be able to write to her neglectful son and daughter-in-law. But I do not write to people unless they have first written to me, tempting as it often is. It would be an impertinent intrusion.

Loneliness means different things to different people. To young men and women it can simply mean not having anyone to go out with, more than once or twice a week. To the young bed-sitter population of London and the other big cities it means night after night of gloomy imprisonment in a narrow environment.

I am amazed by the large number of young people who tell me they have no opportunity to meet others in their age group. The fact is that the opportunities exist, but the lonely young lack the confidence to grasp them.

'How do I begin a conversation?' they write. Or 'If I force myself to go anywhere where I'll meet people, I can never think of anything to say to them.' Or, jokily, 'I must have BO or bad breath or the plague or something – the way people leave me alone.'

I explain that huge numbers of people lack self-confidence and the chances are that many of her contemporaries are as shy as the tongue-tied girl. Or that the boy who is terrified of a snub if he approaches a girl, is as shy as the girl herself. I suggest conversational gambits – ask leading questions. Ask him – or her – about himself, about his job or his hobbies, where he went for his holidays or where he's going. I give examples of what NOT to say. Like 'Did you enjoy your holiday?' This sort of question produces a flat bleak yes or no from a shy citizen. And although I am none too optimistic that simple tips like this can help to unleash a flood of sparkling conversation, I've had letters back from girls and boys saying such ploys helped to get them started in new friendships.

Boys, curiously, seem to have even more difficulty in com municating than girls. It's heartbreaking to read a letter from a young man who is unable to talk to girls, who has never had a girl friend. He painfully watches the ease with which his friends meet girls, make dates, get engaged, while he alone finds that talking to a girl naturally is as impossible as flying to the moon. Is there, he wants to know, some hidden magic formula, some easily learned technique which will make him relaxed, communicative and interesting to the opposite sex instead of tongue-tied, nervous and shy?

Q. I've just come home from the local disco and as usual I've come home alone. All my friends have taken home the girls they met, or their steadies. For the umpteenth time my evening has been a disaster.

I am eighteen and as yet I haven't had a girl friend let alone a sexual experience. I am not much to look at, being very thin and I am also short-sighted and have to wear glasses. Sometimes I manage to start talking to girls but I think they laugh at me behind my back. I wonder if I'll ever find someone.

A. I think you are looking in the wrong place when you look for love in a disco. The very atmosphere of a disco is inhibiting and you can hardly call the exchange of shouts and screams above the noise conversation.

From your description of yourself, you don't sound like the sort of boy who would be at his best in such highly competitive places. I'm sure you'd do much better in clubs geared to special interests. Like drama groups or sports clubs. I don't know what your interests are, but if you enquire at your library, they'll give you a list of local activities.

A lot of young people who, like you, lack confidence in themselves, take up Youth Voluntary Work. Not only do they do a worthwhile job for the community, but they make lots of friends.

Forget about being thin and wearing specs. Once you find friends, they won't notice how you look. Right now, you are so sensitive about your appearance, you convince yourself that girls think it's funny. I doubt if they do. I'm sure you imagine it simply because you're trying to find a reason why the girls leave you alone. Stay away from discos and search where you'll have a very good chance of success.

Young people who lack the confidence to make friends and relationships in their teens often find it becomes increasingly difficult as they get older. Schoolfriends and acquaintances marry and drift out of touch, leaving their lonely contemporaries more and more isolated so that they retreat into the closed family circle, where they feel safe.

Q. I never got on well with the other girls at school and ever since, I've shrunk away from people more and more. Now, at twenty-eight, I still live with my parents. I do not seem to be able to talk to people, especially men. I try to make conversation but it always goes wrong somehow or I say something stupid. Whenever I am in company, I seem to make a fool of myself. I feel safe living with my parents. I work in a small office, but I am desperately lonely. I would love to get on with others and have some real friends.

A. There are very few human beings so totally self-assured that they are never secretly fearful of making idiots of themselves. You, like everyone, must have a self-image, a picture of the sort of person you believe yourself to be underneath the shy and withdrawn person you publicly present.

Perhaps this self-image was once battered. At school, maybe, or at work. Someone may have hurt you – and you could well have forgotten the incident. Sensitive people often retreat into a shell of their own making for fear of another battering until, in the end, they have actually almost buried their self-image in a desire to protect it from further harm. To gain confidence, the hidden image must be encouraged to emerge.

It's no comfort to you if I tell you that many of the people you long to be able to talk to also lack the confidence which is making you so unhappy. The main difference is, perhaps, that they have learned to put on an act as a cover-up.

You feel safe with your parents who aren't going to hurt you. But you feel very unsafe indeed with anyone else who might.

Next time you're in company, try not to talk at all. Let others do the talking. You just listen and listen intelligently and don't attempt to participate unless you have something worthwhile to contribute. The chances are that you will have, if you pay more attention to what others are saying and doing and less to rehearsing your few halting words. Good listeners are as rare and valuable as gold bars.

It is widows and divorcees, though, who make up most of the numbers of people who write about loneliness; knowing how to fill the void left by the loss of a loved one and to start afresh presents them with insurmountable problems.

Two factors have greatly increased loneliness among women who are neither young nor very elderly: the incidence of earlier deaths among men, and the fact that women have a longer life expectancy. The soaring divorce and separation rate have left many women and a considerable number of men with a special problem of loneliness.

I estimate that about a million people come into this category and my estimate is, I think, a conservative one, based on the Finer One-Parent Family Committee's 1972 estimate of 600,000 lone-parents. And Finer was only looking at lone people with children; there is a large number of divorced, separated or widowed people who are childless or whose teenage children no longer need support.

Women in the forty to fifty age group tell me that the men they meet are not interested in a regular commitment. Men see them as easy game, use them for a casual sexual romp while they're searching for younger women to marry or to live with. Most of the men they meet in their age group are, in any case, married. One thirty-nine-year-old widow wrote bitterly, 'Married men regard you as light entertainment on the side. Men who are free want girls of 20.' Many women write along these lines. . . .

Q. I never have any trouble attracting men (it sounds boastful, but it's true) but I can't manage to keep them interested for more than a few weeks.

I've been assured by many that I am very attractive, even at forty-two. I've got the right statistics and a sense of humour, so what's wrong? Why do eligible men disappear as soon as you say you like them and would like to develop a regular relationship? Oh, the married ones are keen enough, especially about getting into bed, but the single ones leave me flat in no time at all. I was divorced last year and desperately long to settle down again with a decent, steady man.

A. It appears to me that you frighten off the men who would be most likely to stay the course. I think they hear warning bells, which sound to them dangerously like wedding bells. It is well known that most men flee in terror if they believe a trap is being laid for them. If you allow your dreams of domesticity to creep into the conversation, the men to whom you reveal them are likely to see them as nightmares of mortgages and depleted bank balances.

A man in love would share your dreams, but you've got to

give love a chance to grow. I suspect that by now, you've become so anxious to remarry that plainly it shows. You use the word 'desperately'. Maybe the men you meet feel they're your last desperate chance. Instead of regarding every new male who moves into your orbit as a potential husband, it might pay off if you could regard him as a pleasant friend. Push those dreams into the back of your mind for they'll never come true if you will insist on revealing them. It will help you to appear, at any rate, to be less desperate.

Many clubs have sprung up in recent years to meet the needs of the divorced and separated and they are valuable in helping people to build up a fresh social life. But they are heavily unbalanced with women outnumbering men by an average of about five to one. Even so a good many people lack the confidence to join them and, as they so often tell me, they force themselves to go once or twice and give up when success eludes them. I explain that even if they don't start an association with someone of the opposite sex, they will widen their circle and find, at least, some companionship.

Q. I have been a widow for five lonely years. Gradually, my friends have almost disappeared, for a woman alone is not very welcome among married couples. My daughter is trying to persuade me to join a club where, she says, I will meet others like myself. I am in my late fifties and would like to marry again – or at any rate, to meet a man around my age who would be a pleasant companion. But I have heard that at these clubs nearly all the members are women. I've never come across any couples who have met at a club, have you? Also, I think I'd feel a bit of a fool joining one.

A. It's perfectly true that the sort of clubs you're thinking of usually have many more women members than men. Just the same, I've heard of plenty of autumnal romances among the not-so-young who've met at clubs – or through them. For the fact is that when you join one, you widen your circle of friends and this can sometimes have an indirect advantage.

4

One lady I know met her intended at his sister's home –
and she'd met the sister at a club. I had news only the other
day of an impressive score of four weddings and five engage-
ments all recently started at a group which meets in a
London suburb. Don't imagine you'll feel a fool joining a
club. Remember, all the other members are in a similar
situation – seeking friendship and love.

Many people insert ads in the lonely hearts columns of
magazines and have chalked up successes. One notable instance
is the distinguished artist John Bratby, who gave me permission
to publish his name. He wrote to me about his reactions to meeting a woman in what he described as these unconventional
circumstances. I expressed some surprise that a man as well
known as he is, with, surely, many opportunities for contact
with women should need to resort to a lonely hearts ad column.
But he assured me that he was desperately lonely after the break-
up of his marriage and that he had very few chances to meet
someone else. He also remarked that, although the end results
were satisfactory, at the beginning of his association with
the woman he met, their behaviour was stilted, awkward and
unnatural. It was over a year before they could relax and he felt
that the slow development of the relationship was entirely due
to the unconventional way it began.

When readers ask my views about introductions through
advertisements, introduction agencies or marriage bureaux, I
warn them of possible disappointments. But then, as I point out,
meeting someone in more conventional circumstances can
equally result in disappointment. The virtue of introduction
agencies is that most of those who use their services are earnestly
seeking partners; everyone is in the same lonely boat and the
following letter from a man illustrates how even someone
personable and, it appears, sociable, is unable to meet suitable
women.

Q. A year ago my wife left me for another man, taking the
children with her. I was shattered and broken-hearted and at
first I thought I would never get over it. I even contemplated

suicide. However, as time has gone by I have been able to face up to it with a little more equanimity. I go out for the occasional drink and mix easily enough with men in pubs, but the women who go to pubs singly or in pairs are more like casual pick-ups than possible partners.

I would dearly like to meet a nice woman near my age. I am in my late thirties and not unattractive. I have no close friends who would introduce me to women, so my life is very empty and dull.

A. It is with a certain amount of hesitation that I am going to suggest to you that you register with a marriage bureau or introduction agency. My hesitation is based on the suspicion I have that you are a rather conventional man and may reject the idea as being distasteful. But many people in circumstances similar to yours have made successful relationships in this way and I think you should seriously consider my suggestion.

You will know that women to whom you are introduced are as anxious as you are to find a partner. Do not imagine that all the women who register at marriage or introduction bureaux are misfits. Most, like yourself, are unable to meet suitable partners because they lack opportunities to do so.

The sort of women you meet in pubs, the easy pick-ups, are not going to provide you with the companionship you seek. But registering with a bureau, you will have the opportunity of expressing your preferences. You will have a chance to meet women who share your interests, whose background and life style coincide with your own.

You must be prepared for disappointments, even, perhaps, for rejection – just as you will be free to reject anyone who fails to attract you. You must be patient and not expect immediate results. If you should be lucky enough to meet an ideal woman, do not rush into a commitment simply because you are both lonely and in need of affection. Get to know each other. Wait long enough to shake off the awkwardness that may well be the result of meeting in the way I have suggested. Go to a well-established bureau with a good reputation.

It will cost you money – it can cost quite a lot – but for you it would, I think, be the best possible investment for the future.

Some of the lonely people who write to me experience severe sexual frustration, particularly the women who are either un-willing or lack opportunity for the casual sexual fulfilment which would temporarily ease their frustrations. Again, it is easier, generally, for men to find relief for these particular tensions but many women, living isolated lives, have no outlet. This applies particularly to young women with children and to women who have had a sexually fulfilling relationship, brought to an abrupt end when a partner dies or deserts them.

Q. My husband died a year ago. I loved him very much and now I am so lost and lonely, I can't describe my feelings. If it wasn't for my baby daughter I'd have nothing to make life worth living. The nights are the worst times and I have to admit that sometimes I feel so desperately frustrated and alone that I masturbate. Though it gives me some sort of pleasure, and relief for a while, I always feel guilty and sordid after. It's taken a lot of courage to write and tell you this, but I hope you understand. Is what I do wrong or harmful?

A. I do understand and I understand why you felt you needed courage to write. But I'm very glad you were brave for it gives me the chance to try to reassure you. Masturba-tion is neither wrong nor harmful. Tiny babies do it, as do children and adults. When there is no other way of gaining sexual relief this is a substitute which helps. Of course, it's not ideal sex, which needs two people to make it complete and rewarding, but it's better for a lot of people than nothing at all. For you especially, it's a little consolation and you must stop thinking of it as sordid. You must certainly stop feeling guilty. No need to – for who are you harming? Certainly neither yourself nor anyone else. Perhaps, one of these days, you will find consolation with a new partner – and life, every facet of it – will once again be very well worth living. Meanwhile, there is no reason why you should not continue the practice which eases the frustration you naturally feel.

*

Q. I am a young divorcee aged thirty-three – and am tormented by sexual desires. I have no children and I go out with a few men and have plenty of opportunity for sexual satisfaction. Men tell me they find me attractive and they want to make love to me. But so far I have resisted, for I have always believed that sex without love is debased and meaningless. Women friends say I am foolish and old-fashioned not to have a good time and I wonder if they're right.

A. I don't think, really, that sex has much to do with fashion. It has to do with attitudes which I suppose involve contemporary thinking and behaviour. For a lot of people, sex is little more than a release of frustration and if you were one of these people, I'd say go ahead – so long as your partners are as free as you are.

It would be a very bad idea to get into bed with a married man just to get rid of your torments. But you clearly do not see sex in the same light as, say, regularly brushing your teeth. It has more than just a physical significance to you, and for that reason I say to you that you would be wise to ignore your friends' advice. If you feel that sex without love is meaningless, it would never be good for you – however satisfactory it was at the time of the action. It would leave you with a feeling of 'So what?'

At thirty-three, you are certainly young enough and it seems interesting enough, to attract men. Wait awhile in the hope that one turns up whose attitude matches yours.

You don't always have to be a single person to be lonely. Even wives with devoted husbands write to say how lonely they are.

(It's interesting that I cannot recall a letter from the lonely husband of a devoted wife.)

The loneliest wives are women married to men who leave them alone night after night – men who prefer to drink with friends rather than stay home with their wives, men who pursue hobbies which exclude their wives, men who work long hours or who work at night. Even women whose husbands are physically present in the home complain of the loneliness of life with a man who either dozes in front of the TV, buries himself behind newspapers or escapes to the garage to tinker with the car.

It is tempting to encourage such wives to take up hobbies of their own but this is not always a practical solution, for most of them have children. In any case, to suggest to a wife that she, too, ought to go out and find amusement without her husband is dangerous. Such advice could result in a broken marriage and while I sometimes feel that the sort of marriages these wives describe are hollow and are potentially at risk, I feel that for many women in middle age, even an unsatisfactory marriage is better than no marriage at all.

Sometimes women have written to say their loneliness has driven them to leave their husbands – and they describe how they've lived to regret their decision. The only comfort I can offer such wives is to remind them that a man tinkering with his car or drinking with his men friends is, at any rate, not engaging in the hobby so many men pursue: chasing other women. It is small comfort.

But a lot of the complaining wives could do much more to alleviate their loneliness. Too many of them, dependent on their husbands for companionship, see them as the cause of their loneliness and make no effort to haul themselves out of their isolation.

Q. We recently moved from a big industrial city to a small village. We have a lovely little house, the village is perfect, the children (six and eight) are happy and so is my husband, who commutes every day to his office. But I have never been so miserable in my life. I feel like a foreigner. The people in the village are unfriendly, and I am so lonely I'm going out of my mind. Sometimes I don't speak to a soul all day except the milkman. I'm beginning to drive my husband crazy, too, nagging at him the minute he gets in. He has said we can move back to town if I'm really unhappy, but we can't afford to do that and I'd feel even worse about uprooting the children again. Do you think we'd be wise to move back?

A. No. I think you'd be wise to take steps to get yourself accepted by this aloof little community. To them you are a foreigner, idiotic as it may sound. But once you get through to them, they'll begin to realise you're just the same as they are. So brace yourself to make the first move. Maybe you could get to know some of the other mothers through your children. Give a children's party and their mothers are bound to fetch and carry their offspring. Then ask the mothers to tea. Join a women's group – or a charity organisation. You will just have to be a bit pushy at first, until you break down their reserve. It's ridiculous that a stranger in a village has to woo the natives but once you've won them over, I am sure you'll be sold on country-style living.

It is hardly fair – and, indeed, it's very foolish – to victimise your husband. You cannot rely on him exclusively to provide you with the companionship you need. You must help yourself, otherwise you will never escape from your loneliness and you could, in fact, end up even lonelier if your nagging drives your husband away.

An extreme example of a woman unable to face up to loneliness is demonstrated in this letter. . . .

Q. I have just about sobered up enough to write this letter. I'm forty-six years old and, until a year ago, was a fairly attractive woman, I think. Anyway, I always made the best of myself. Now I'm just a mess – in every way. It began when my husband left me for a girl younger than our daughter. I know I am weak, that many women would have coped, but I couldn't. I started drinking because I was so lonely and desperate and couldn't sleep thinking of him with this girl. Now I am just a disintegrating human being, but in my sober moments, I long to get back my self-respect and my looks and try to live like a normal person again. I have no friends left – only one really who cares about me and her husband has now told her to stay away from me. What can I do? Help me please, if you can bring yourself not to despise me.

A. Believe me – I do not despise you. I feel deeply sorry for you. In fact, of course, you despise yourself and it's much harder to cope with self-dislike than with other people's dislike. If others are critical, you can shrug and say they can go to hell – and you can ignore their contempt. But when the contempt is of yourself, you cannot ignore it. All you can do is have another swig at the bottle in an attempt to forget how much you hate what you've become.

I am sure I don't have to tell you that the more you drink to forget, the harder it will be for you even to remember how once you were attractive and desirable. You know that – in your sober moments. And while you still have a few sober moments, and before time runs out and your life is irrevocably wrecked, you must take steps to get help. I cannot personally do more than assure you it's never too late for an alcoholic like you to be rescued – and because you *want* to be rescued, you can be.

There is an organisation, Alcoholics Anonymous, which could help you. I know of countless people they've saved from despair. They cannot wave a magic wand and get you sober overnight. But they can help you to fight back to regain that self-respect you long for. Stay sober long enough to dial their number. Once you've made contact, the sober times won't be so few and far between.

Perhaps one of the most poignant letters I have ever received from a lonely citizen is this one, which seems to me to sum up the sadness of loneliness and isolation.

q. I have developed a habit that is worrying me. Since my husband left me six months ago for another woman, I have lived alone in our suburban house. My only son is married. Recently I've realised that I am talking aloud to myself. Sometimes, when the radio is on, I find myself answering back at it.

I mutter to myself in the mornings about what the weather is like and what to wear. I'm beginning to get quite frightened. How can I conquer this habit before it gets out of hand?

A. Please try not to worry about this habit you've developed. It's perfectly understandable. When you've lived with someone for years and you're suddenly bereft of your companion, the chatter which was part of marriage is silenced, the silence can be thunderous.

I know that when I've had to go away from home and have stayed alone in hotels, sometimes for weeks, I, too, have found myself asking myself aloud whether to wear my green or my pink or whatever. I recall doing just this once in New York when the waiter came in with my breakfast. He looked very suspiciously round my single room and glanced in the bathroom on the way out, clearly certain I was concealing someone in it.

I won't suggest you'll grow accustomed, in time, to being alone. But I hope you'll manage to come to terms with it. Meanwhile, it doesn't matter if you do argue with disembodied radio voices, or acknowledge the pleasant 'good evening' of the TV newscasters. Lots of people do. But here is a practical suggestion to alleviate your loneliness: couldn't you let a room? It would be nice to have a couple of students or nurses, for instance, making cheerful noises around the house. Or another lonely person who'd be as grateful as you to have someone with whom to discuss the weather.

Parenthood: Pain or Pleasure?

From our earliest days, we are geared to a formal pattern of education. We begin by learning to read and write, to tell the time, to use a knife and fork, to add up and subtract. We are taught history and geography, maths and French and biology and how to play football and netball. We are trained in shorthand and typing, engineering, law, architecture, medicine or bricklaying. We are conditioned, from the moment we utter our first lisping words, to learn. We are carefully prepared by our educators to absorb lessons necessary to our development, lessons which will provide us with the skills we will need to pay the rent, clothe and feed ourselves and our families. The one vital subject missing from the curriculum is parenthood.

In the same way that many people naively believe that sex is something which comes naturally, they assume that parenthood also comes naturally. It is one of the most dangerous myths of out time. It is a myth responsible for an amount of misery which cannot be estimated.

Certain parental instincts are, indeed, natural. It is natural to animals to protect their young and the majority of humans share this primitive instinct. Love and caring too are natural instincts, as are feeding, sheltering and comforting the young. Pride in one's offspring is also a natural parental instinct and all these together are part of the powerful nesting urge which, in broad terms, humans and animals share.

But instinct alone is not enough in our complex society to maintain an ideal relationship between parents and their offspring. Even those parents who, aware of the gap in education for parenthood, try to approach its problems rationally and intelligently, discover that theory doesn't measure up in practice. They may read learned books on child psychology while their infant is still in the womb, but when it emerges, they discover that the product of their coupling is a character in its own right, a mixture of generations of genes and hormones not made in their own image.

I know child psychologists who are just as baffled when it comes to rearing their own children as are any less well informed parents. There is a distinguished consultant in child psychiatry at one of our leading hospitals, for instance, who has daunting problems with his own two children. His wife is a teacher. They are both 'good' parents; yet their problems with their children are, he tells me, just as difficult as those he meets in his work. He believes that closing the gap in education for parenthood would help but wouldn't entirely cure the ills which beset this trickiest of relationships.

Both parents and children are subjected to and influenced by social, economic and psychological pressures outside the family circle. There are deep-seated, ingrained attitudes based on custom, on religion, on prejudice and intolerance, on repression of the natural instincts. There are heavy sexual undertones in parent-child relationships creating conflicts which are passed from generation to generation. And there are social conflicts which complicate the deeper issues.

Are today's parenthood problems greater than they were? This is a question I am often asked and it is a hard one to answer. Certainly I receive more letters relating to these problems than I did twenty years ago. But this is hardly a valid yardstick; people are more aware of *all* problems now. Or, at any rate, more ready to discuss them and to seek help in resolving them.

Many sociologists believe that the breakdown of close family life is largely responsible for the breakdown in the parent-child relationship. The working mother comes under heavy fire. The old, cosy idea of the woman as the pivot of the home, with her children gathered about her, always there to give them security, maintaining a tender discipline, the home permeated with the mixed domestic smells of baking and beeswax has all but vanished. The home where father came in at the end of the day to find his rosily clean children in bed, the bedtime story read by their tranquil mother, the evening meal on the stove, is now as unreal as that bedtime fairytale. Perhaps it was never quite as real as we've been led to believe. But this nostalgia for family life, Victorian style, is a nostalgia for a middle-class society which must only have existed for the few; there have always, I don't doubt, been neglected children, rejected children, unloved and unwanted children, bad parents, indifferent parents, selfish parents.

Nevertheless, the working-mother syndrome must, I believe, contribute to many of the problems faced by today's parents. There is, at the very least, a terrible dilemma for women, pressured on the one hand to be equal and independent, to fulfil their career potential, to contribute to the family's finances and on the other, to stay at home and fulfil their biological role of motherhood.

I faced the dilemma myself when my only son was six years old. 'Why,' he asked me, when I was for some now-forgotten reason home from the office at tea-time, 'aren't you like other mummies? Why don't you stay at home and make my cucumber sandwiches for tea?' His cucumber sandwiches were made by the mother's help who met him from school, played with him and bathed him – the surrogate mother who cared for him until I rushed in from work breathlessly to read the bedtime story he waited up for.

His question brought out into the open the anxiety I'd wrestled with since his birth. Luckier than many mothers, I'd been able to work at home during his first five years, often working far into the night so as to be able to devote myself to him during the day. But I always knew I would pursue a career. And knew I would suffer the same doubts, the same guilt other mothers write to me about today.

That day, which became fixed in my mind as cucumber-sandwich day, was my particular moment of truth. 'Should I give up my job?' I asked my husband, prodding him awake at intervals during my sleepless night. 'Should I stay home and make sandwiches and be a full-time mother?' My husband said it must be my decision but he asked me a few questions to help me to try to clarify my confused mind.

'Will you be a better mother if you stay home? will you get impatient and grow resentful towards the child who prevents you from doing what you want to do? will he be enriched by the wider, broader life you'll lead if you work – or impoverished by it? will the inevitable guilt make you over-indulge and over-compensate him for your absence?' They were impossible questions to answer. 'Who knows?' I kept repeating to myself.

In the years that followed, as my son grew old enough for discussions, I asked him whether he thought his life had been richer or poorer because of my job. Richer, he thinks. He believes I would have been unhappy and frustrated and that it would have rebounded on him. He believes – and I agree with him – that a woman must choose, as long as her children aren't physically or emotionally neglected and know they are loved and wanted and feel secure. And so the cucumber sandwiches, for so many years a symbol of guilt and doubt, have now become a family joke and when he visits me with his two children, he says, 'Cucumber sandwiches for tea, I suppose.'

I have been lucky to be able to communicate with my son from his earliest days, throughout his school life and adolescent life and now, his married life. We have an easy companionship. We argue often, quarrel sometimes, but we respect each other. Not all parents are as fortunate.

In some cases, communication between parents and children breaks down when the children reach puberty; in some families there's no chance of communication breaking down for it never existed in the first place. As one young mother said to me, 'It's all very well for people to talk all this rubbish about com-municating with young children. I sometimes wonder if they've ever had any. You try carrying on a conversation day in and day out with a couple of toddlers. It's not exactly rewarding. And when they drive you mad with their fighting and pee-ing on the floor and wrecking the place, talking isn't going to get you any-where. You put them in the garden or stick them in front of the TV just to keep them quiet, just to have a bit of peace and get your housework done.'

It's easy to see why women like this are scornful of high-minded, do-gooding advice to 'communicate'. 'For God's sake get out of my sight and shut up', is the usual one-sided conversation, accompanied by yells of protest from the furious offspring. And it's easy enough for lofty experts to be critical of such mothers.

It would help, I suggest to them, to spend more time reading to children, for TV has taken over from the afternoon and evening story-book session which provided a close loving link, physical and emotional as well as mental. Of course it's less trouble to switch on the telly and plonk the kids in front of it than to spend time reading but time spent during babyhood and pre-school days is a sure investment for the future of the relationship.

When children begin to ask the questions which perturb many parents, it's the parents who have learned how to talk to their children who are most easily able to supply answers. A good many parents begin to realise their conversational limitations when children start school and come home asking questions about sex. Some parents think teachers should supply the answers; others, aware of their parental responsibilities, write and say, 'What do I tell them, and how do I do it?'

Sex cannot be taught to children in a vacuum as an isolated subject. It must be part of the whole spectrum of learning about attitudes towards others, about concern and about the sharing of responsibilities. Teachers can instruct children in biological subjects; parents, by example and by demonstrating their own good attitudes, can teach them much more. The trouble is that parents have their own neuroses and their own ignorance to contend with. The large majority of the letters I receive from parents demonstrates ignorance and inhibition. Curiously, fathers are often more puritan-minded than mothers. . . .

Q. My wife is determined that our daughter, aged six, and son, aged nine, shall be brought up to know that sex is a good natural function and that there's nothing nasty about nudity. I agree with her in principle, but am getting tired of the total lack of privacy in our home. My kids barge in and out while

I'm in the bath, wander into the bedroom when I'm dressing – or undressing – looking at me with a kind of frank appraisal. My wife, whose privacy is, of course, also invaded, takes it gaily in her stride but it's beginning to bother me and I have asked her to put a limit to their bed and bathroom invasions. She accuses me of being a hypocrite – preaching but not wanting to practise.

A. You could be justly accused of illogical behaviour if you support your wife's theories about the children's upbringing but draw a veil – or bath towel – over the realities. I wonder why you've become so self-conscious. Is it because you are aware that the children you probably regarded as innocent babies are beginning to be sexually alert?

It can hardly be curiosity which makes them stare so appraisingly, for if they've been ambling unrestricted through bathroom and bedroom since toddler-hood, they must by now be quite accustomed to your unclad form. And I'd have thought you'd be so used to their casual wanderings that you'd take their presences as much for granted as you take, say, your shaver.

I think you should ask yourself why you've begun to find it all so tiresome and why you suddenly yearn for privacy and if you come up with a valid reason, you should express it to your wife. She sounds eminently sensible.

It would, I think, be damaging to your children, to your relationship with them and to peace and harmony in the home if you began locking doors now. You could set up in them a lot of inhibitions your healthy-minded wife is trying to avoid.

Numerous parents write similar letters to this one. . . .

Q. My six-year-old daughter asked me why she didn't have 'sex dedication' lessons at her school. When my husband and I had stopped laughing, we wondered if it wouldn't be a bad idea to explain one or two minor points, even though she is a bit muddled about the words. Is six too young to start?

A. She certainly thinks she's missing out on something: perhaps some of her mature friends of eight or nine have told her sex dedication is much more interesting than sums. The age to tell children is when they start seeking information. Yours is showing enough interest for you to impart a few simple facts.

Tell her in simple language how babies grow in the uterus and how they get there. Explain how the father's sperm fertilises the mother's egg and how the seed grows into a baby. Tell her it happens because the father and mother love each other and want to be very close together to have the baby to love too. But be careful not to bore the child. As soon as her attention wanders, stop the lesson. She'll ask more questions when she's ready.

*

Q. I am a widow with an eight-year-old son and have never spoken to him about sex. However, one of my neighbours tells me that my son has been seen exposing himself to little girls and although I know that I must speak to him, I just don't know how to begin.

A. Try not to worry or to take this youthful exposure too seriously. Most children do this. It's simply an expression of interest in their bodies and a sudden realisation among little boys that they've got different equipment from little girls and are rather proud of their additional endowment.

The best way to cope is to explain the structural differences between boys and girls – and then to tell him that it's polite behaviour to keep private parts of the body covered up. You can say that although there is nothing whatever to be ashamed of about bodies, people usually prefer to keep them covered up when there are strangers about. Don't be cross with him and make him feel guilty or give him the impression that exposing himself is nasty or dirty.

Some mothers are tempted to tell little boys that the sort of thing he's been doing is rather like going to the lavatory and leaving the door open. I'm opposed to this line of argument. It identifies sexuality with bodily functions that have unclean associations. Just keep calm and be matter-of-fact and say that other children know what he's got and there's no further need to continue to uncover the mystery. Then give him a hug and a present to take his mind off what's inside his knickers and I hope your mind will consequently be at ease.

The major problem faced by parents of older children is the ever-widening gap between them from puberty onwards. It's during this period that nervous parents strengthen discipline – and teenagers revolt against it. Many parents fail to realise that it's necessary to respect their children's feelings and their search for individuality. But anti-social behaviour shouldn't go unchallenged.

There's a big difference between repressiveness and sensitive tolerance. It's dangerous for parents to demand that their children are their own mirror-images. This interesting letter typifies such parental attitudes. . . .

Q. I am so ashamed of my son that I have agreed to my husband's banning him from the house unless he pulls himself together. He is scruffy, dirty and his tangled hair reaches his shoulders. We have done everything for him, have given him a wonderful home and the best school we could afford.

Last year he was sent down from university and he promptly took off hitch-hiking round Europe. He probably smokes pot. He's penniless. He is rude to us and insulting about our friends who, he says, don't give a damn about anyone but themselves. We are well respected and you can imagine how deeply hurt we feel. Our daughter is completely the opposite, married to an architect with a lovely family. Why does he behave like this? How can children be so ungrateful?

A. There are countless sons answering closely to the description of yours, and breaking their parents' hearts. You are deeply disappointed in him. But has it ever occurred to you that he may be equally disappointed in you and his father? You are concerned about his appearance, his indifference to your decent standards. They are standards he has rejected because, like so many of his contemporaries (of both sexes) he finds them shallow and lacking in the values he admires.

People like your son despise materialism. They are sickened by what they believe is an unfair distribution of the world's riches. They go overboard to look as different from their parents as they can in order to show their hatred of middle-class standards. Until you understand this, you will never narrow the gap between you and your boy.

As for expecting gratitude from children: why should parents demand gratitude? It always puzzled me that so many do. We have them, love them, get endless delight and much sorrow from them, do the best we can for them and hope they'll love us forever. But we shouldn't be looking for their grateful thanks. Sometimes, I think we should thank our children for opening our eyes and stirring our conscience. For boys like your son may not care for the joys of suburban life, but they do care deeply about the under-privileged peoples of the world. And you'd be surprised at how much they do to help them in their scruffy, off-beat way.

The major disciplinarian role in the family is the mother's, with the rather shadowy father in the background upheld as the ultimate head of the household. Skirmishes over clothes, shoes, hair, money and boy friends frequently never reach him so it is hardly surprising that most of the conflicts are directly between the mother and child. As a result, the majority of the letters on the subject of children come from mothers. From about fifteen years old upwards, children's relationships with the opposite sex cause the greatest concern and the bulk of my mail in this area is to do with sex.

Q. Until recently, our fifteen-year-old daughter has never

given us any problems, but now, she is completely obsessed by sex. She seemed such an innocent child, but I have found stories she's written describing the sex act in detail, as if she's got first-hand knowledge, and her room is scattered with lurid magazines.

When she was about ten, she asked me questions about sex and I explained it all to her in a matter-of-fact way and she never raised the subject again. I am very worried about this obsession and I do not know how to handle it. Her father shrugs and says it's a normal part of growing up, but is it?

A. You must try to put this matter into perspective and realise that your daughter's behaviour is, in fact, perfectly normal. She is becoming consciously aware of her sexuality and her need for some sort of expression of it. The explicit stories she writes and the magazines she reads are simply an outlet for her sexual fantasies.

It's lucky there's no evidence that she's indulged her dreams beyond reading and writing. Many parents discover, with horror, that their innocent-seeming young daughters act out their sexual fantasies with boys – and not simply on paper. I expect this is your chief worry. I know you feel you did your duty when you answered her questions five years ago. It's a pity the dialogue stopped so abruptly and has never been resumed and I think you ought to start it up again – cautiously.

All too often a teenager will write to me saying, 'I can't talk to my mother about sex or boys.' It would be splendid if your daughter felt she could rely on you to listen under-standingly.

She's going through that troublesome time which I call teenage sexual limbo, moving clumsily from childhood into womanhood. You can't expect her to leap the gap and change overnight from a little girl to a mature woman. All you can do is help her over it, as kindly as a loving mother can.

✳

Q. I have discovered that my daughter is sleeping with her boy friend. I am terribly upset, for she is only just eighteen and he is not yet twenty. So far as I know, they have no thought of marriage. In fact, she has told me that she doesn't intend to marry until she's got her degree. I am very distressed to discover they are having intercourse. I do not know what to do. My husband is no help – he is always hiding behind his newspaper when there is anything serious to discuss. Should I tackle her – or the boy?

A. Today's parents (even your husband cowering behind his newspaper) have to accept the fact that their teenage children have a much more permissive attitude to sex than they had. You probably did your share of petting in the back of your boy friend's car. But you didn't go the whole way. Maybe if you had been pretty sure you'd be safe from an unwanted pregnancy, you might have gone further. Don't be angry with me for saying this. Be realistic, not hypocritical. Ask yourself if you want your daughter to marry at eighteen, before she is sure she loves the man, before she has completed her education – simply in order to enjoy 'legal' sex.

I am not trying to make out a case for 'illegal' sex, but just looking at the situation from a practical angle. Indeed, I would be as anxious as you are in the circumstances. But I hope I'd see things as they are and not merely as I'd like them to be.

I advise you to talk to your girl about the dangers of sex without emotional involvement and the potential misery of giving birth to an unplanned or unwanted baby. Having said your piece, join your husband and keep quiet. Your daughter is legally entitled to make her own decisions. If you try to block her freedom, she'll probably leave home to get away from what she'd consider an intrusion into her privacy. It's sad. But it's a fact of teenage life.

Parents never stop worrying about their children and trying to organise their lives, even when those children have become adults. It would be easy for me to write to such parents and tell them briskly to stop interfering, but I am filled with compassion for people who see their sons and daughters taking what they see as destructive actions. For as both children and parents grow older, the gap between them can widen into a chasm which cannot be bridged. Which is why I try to get parents to loosen the knots as gently as possible. . . .

Q. I have been a widow for many years and am deeply worried about my only son, aged twenty-four. He has fallen in love with a married woman of thirty-three who has two children and is separated from her husband. This couple were living apart when my son met the woman. My boy has said he intends to move into her flat. He loves the children and believes that he and this woman can live happily as man and wife, despite the difference in their age. He has just qualified as an accountant and I am afraid this association will ruin his life.

A. It is probably because you have no husband that your son has fallen in love with this girl. A boy brought up by a mother alone would be quite likely to seek out an older woman. He is accustomed to love from an older woman. I dare say you have done everything possible to make up to him for being fatherless and in a way, his feeling for this girl is a compliment to you. He likes being mothered.

Of course he'd be taking on a good deal of responsibility with a ready-made family but he isn't a thoughtless headstrong youth, not if he's the stuff of which accountants are made. They usually know how to balance things up and he's probably done a profit and loss account and decided that he'll get more profit than loss out of the arrangement. I do not think the age difference should give you cause for worry. I have known many good relationships where there is a big gap.

You may, perhaps, secretly be hoping that because of the very impermanence of the relationship – since they cannot marry – your son will be free to leave if things go wrong. I can't stop you wishing but I hope I can use a little influence to prevent you from expressing the fact to him or her. Give them your blessing and do all you can to act like the nice mother-in-law you will be, in everything except the law.

This small selection of letters about the problems of parenthood hardly begins to cover the immensely wide range of anxieties parents write about. Children write too, about their tiresome parents. Young ones (twelve to fourteen) complain that parents insist on ridiculous rules about homecoming times – 'My father says I've got to be home by ten-thirty and all my friends are allowed out until midnight.' Older children accuse their parents of snooping and of invading their privacy, of interfering with friendships, of demanding a too-big share of domestic chores in exchange for pocket money. Girls say their mothers bully them about unsuitable clothes; boys tell of violent quarrels with fathers. Children are clever enough to manipulate their parents to gain their own ends. Parents are foolish enough to use children likewise.

I constantly find myself in the role of a peace-making go-between in this difficult relationship, mainly concerned with trying to get each contestant to see the other's point of view. But since the parent-child relationship is fraught with psychological undercurrents and overlaid with the practical problems of two different generations living under one roof – often in battle conditions – the task of an advice columnist in this field is a particularly difficult one.

As one of my psychiatrist colleagues says, to comfort me when I sometimes despair of being able to help: 'Most children manage to grow up to be adjusted citizens despite their parents.' I only wish they'd manage it *because* of their parents.

Happy Families . . . and Just Good Friends

Whoever invented the game Happy Families was surely indulging in wishful thinking. It is pleasantly comforting to believe that our society is based on the close-knit family circle, of families bound together by love and loyalty, of mothers and fathers and brothers and sisters, grandparents, aunts, uncles, nieces and nephews tied to each other not only by blood, but by warmth and affection.

It is not, however, this charming picture of family life which is exposed to me. Beneath the surface of countless seemingly close-knit family lives, seethe wild currents of jealousy, spite, bitterness and very real dislike. I find myself acting as a referee in family fights; I am asked to pass judgements about where blame should be apportioned; I am expected to pour soothing oil by the gallon on the troubled waters of family life.

Blood, in fact, does not seem to me to be necessarily thicker than water (it's strange how many clichés can be applied to the family). The strong family unit is not, in fact, nearly as solid a structure as it was even a few years ago.

The pattern of young marrieds setting up home round the corner from mum and dad, of granny and grandpa living in the next street and the aunties and uncles within shouting distance is breaking up fast. Young couples tend to move away from the parental environment. Granny is likely to be a still youthful working woman. Uncles and aunts are scattered about, leading their own lives.

Those regular family get-together tea-parties on Sunday afternoons have become almost as rare as the spinster aunt who selflessly devoted her life to her dear sister's offspring.

The break-up of the family as a close unit has, over the years, produced a marked increase in certain problems. Where a young wife could at one time have popped round the corner to talk it over with her mother, as likely as not today, her mother is living in another town, or is at work or is too preoccupied with her own problems. For as families disintegrate, communication between its members vanish and the anxious daughter must seek help from someone else.

Many young women with matrimonial problems which they might, perhaps, have discussed with their mothers now send them to me, though it's true to say that conflicts which marred the mother and daughter relationship while the girl remained unmarried often ease a little when the daughter becomes a wife and joins the 'club' of which all married women automatically become members.

Just the same, a good deal of hostility remains. But the greatest hostility between married women is that which exists between mother-in-law and daughter-in-law. The in-law feud is the most commonplace family problem I am asked to deal with. Two possessive, jealous women, fighting for the loyalty and love of one wretched man is not a pretty sight. The mother-in-law theme which has provided so many stand-up comics with their unfunny material is not a pretty situation.

The rival women go to extraordinary lengths to score points, to vanquish their opponents in the battle for the love of the man they share. Except that they do not see it as sharing. The mother regards his wife as the bitch of a girl who stole him. The wife sees the mother as the bitch of a woman who won't let go.

The tug-of-love man in the middle is the victim of their never-ending war to the death. Even when I am replying to letters from furious daughters-in-law or martyred mothers-in-law, I'm not the least bit hopeful that a few words from me will resolve a problem based on that most fundamental human emotion – jealousy.

Q. I have been married only six months but although I have tried, I cannot get on with my mother-in-law. She never stops reminding me how lucky I was to get her son and implies that he must have been blind to marry me. I am rather plain and ordinary and he is very handsome and I know I'm lucky, but I can't stand the way she rams it down my throat all the time. Have you any advice about shutting her up before I snap back and start a quarrel I know I'll regret? My husband has already told me to stop complaining about his mother, which has hurt me very deeply.

A. Your mother-in-law is typical of many. I'd go so far as to say of most. For whether or not they actually *say* it, they nearly all believe that no girl in the world is good enough for their sons. It's one of those things young wives have to learn to live with. It has nothing to do with your being plain and ordinary and your husband being handsome. Even if he looked like the Hunchback of Notre Dame, his mother would still be convinced that he was the most desirable man in the world. Luckily, you both agree about his desirability and it's good for a girl to have something in common with her mother-in-law.

Do not attempt to stop her flow of praise for the man you both love. Concur with her opinion every time she expresses it. Tell her that not only do you realise how lucky you are to have him but that you're equally lucky to have her. You will be amazed at the bonus this will bring you.

It's said – and it's true – that flattery gets you everywhere. Quarrelling gets you nowhere. Put yourself out to make her your friend, for as an implacable enemy, she can do a good deal of harm to your marriage – and your morale.

An example of the way the hostility between in-laws can be maintained for years is demonstrated in this next letter, which also exposes the immensely difficult problem of what to do about elderly relatives.

Q. My husband and I had to get married because I was pregnant and his mother has always hated me. She has always been convinced that I tricked him into marriage. We have been married for twenty-two years but my mother-in-law has never lost her grudge against me and there have been

terrible quarrels, not only between her and me, but between
me and my husband. She has also been hateful to my
daughter.

Recently my father-in-law died and my husband insists
that his mother must live with us. She is now in her mid-
seventies. I am convinced that if she does come here my
daughter will leave and my marriage will suffer.

A. There is simply no easy solution to the awful dilemma
which confronts you. Either way, you're bound to back a
loser. If you refuse to have your mother-in-law to live with
you, the quarrels with your husband will continue. If you
agree, your life will probably be hell.

I would be dishonest if I said I thought it might work out
if she moved in. It could only work if you were absolutely
determined to make it work, if you could hold your tongue,
ignore her bitter remarks, smile cheerfully when she was
cantankerous and give in to her wishes.

You'd need to be immensely patient and saint-like. But
could you do it? Could you be tolerant enough to put up
with what may well be the comparatively short span of life
left to her?

You are worried about your daughter leaving home, but
she is over twenty-one and bound to leave you soon, either
to marry or to make her own life which, in any case, wouldn't
be such a bad thing. As for quarrelling with your husband,
well I must remind you that it takes two to make a quarrel
and perhaps if he saw you were really trying to make his
mother's last years tolerable, he'd be less hostile and more
sympathetic.

As I write this, I realise I've really leaned towards the
solution you dread. I can only say that faced with a similar
problem, I'd give in and invite the old lady to stay, knowing
only too well the problems I'd face.

You'd have several advantages on your side. You're a lot
younger, you've got a living husband and a home. If you
refuse to have her, you'll suffer not only from your husband's
reproaches but from your own guilt. As I said at the begin-

ning, there's no easy answer. You've got to decide which course will bring the least misery.

I receive as many letters from indignant mothers-in-law as from the wives their sons married. The son is always presented as ideal, a blameless, hard-working, good provider who, in a moment of aberration and temporarily bereft of his usual fine judgement, married a stupid, feckless, lazy, extravagant, heedless slut of a girl.

This letter is typical of thousands I have read. . . .

Q. I have always doubted my daughter-in-law's housekeeping ability. She's fonder of going out and enjoying herself than cooking nourishing meals. Recently, I have noticed that my son is losing weight and looks tired and last time I visited them, I mentioned it to him. My daughter-in-law was furious with me, said there is nothing wrong with her cooking or her husband and rudely suggested I should mind my own business. I was and still am very upset and feel inclined to keep away from them and have nothing more to do with her. But I am anxious about my son and I love him. How should I handle this unhappy situation?

A. You had better begin to handle it with more delicacy and sensitivity than you showed when you mentioned his health in front of your son and his wife. Clearly, she sees in your remarks a criticism of her efficiency as a wife. She leaped to the conclusion that you held her responsible for his peaky look. A natural reaction – and one which put her immediately on the defensive.

Being wise after the event, I must tell you that the sensible thing have done was to have a tactful, friendly woman-to-woman chat about your anxiety. A private phone call to her saying, 'Darling, do you think he looks a bit off colour and might be over-working?' would, I think, have produced better results than the public enquiry. Asking what she thinks is wiser than telling her what you think.

Try to understand her defensive reaction and be tolerant.

Ignore her anger; visit her with a bunch of flowers and say, 'Sorry if I upset you, dear.' I know you're the one who is upset. But you'll be more upset than ever if you don't attempt to heal this breach. If you do, there's a hope she'll say she's worried about your son, too – and even ask your advice about getting him back on form. But I do strongly advise against criticism of her. Your son will get thinner than ever unless you and his wife call a truce.

Another aspect of in-law jealousy is often revealed when a new member is introduced into the family. When brothers marry, for instance, their wives are jealous not only of each other, but of each other's position within the family circle, often starting three- or four-pronged attacks, or sometimes retiring in early martyrdom. So it happens that sisters-in-law write to me about each other's insidious plotting to wheedle their way into family favour. Or they complain that one enjoys special favouritism to the detriment of the other.

I'd often like to knock their silly heads together except that I remember the anguish my own jealousy has caused me from time to time. It's an emotion which is immensely difficult to rationalise. I've known people jealous to the point almost of madness over their pet dog's show of affection for a next-door neighbour. How, then, can I try to steer people away from the disasters brought about by their irrational jealousies?

Q. I have always laughed at women who talk about their spiteful mothers-in-law. Mine has always been wonderful and a real friend – until now. I have been married six years and have two small boys. Recently my husband's brother married a girl who is the cool, beautiful and efficient type. Their house is perfect, she's a great cook and never has a crisis. On the other hand, my home, with two young tearaways, looks lived in, to say the least.

I do a part-time job to help out my teacher husband's salary. We have always been happy, but my mother-in-law has started making comparisons. I am told how marvellous my new sister-in-law is at everything and what good ideas she has about bringing up children. My husband says I'm being absurd and suggests I'm jealous, which is nonsense, but his mother makes me feel like a slut. Should I tell her I find her pointed remarks so hurtful?

A. Of course you are jealous of this perfect sister-in-law. Come on, now, admit it. You resent her efficiency; you resent her for having the leisure to run an orderly household. I dare say it won't be long before she, too, has babies and has to relax her high standards. And I think your resentment of her cool management is being transferred to an exaggerated resentment of your mother-in-law.

You may be convincing yourself that your husband's mother is comparing her sons' wives to your detriment, but I believe your own guilt about your haphazard home is behind it all. Plus that jealousy – understandable when you've held the top spot all these years.

The first thing is to stop feeling guilty. Your family life is happy. I expect your little boys have a great time. Your husband loves you the way you are. I am sure you read more into his mother's remarks than she intends to convey and you'd be wise to ignore them. If you make a big issue of them and confront her with a dramatic scene, you'll lose a friend and create an enemy. Two enemies, in fact, for you are certain to arouse the hostility of your brother-in-law's wife if you stir up trouble in the family. As long as your husband doesn't think of you as a slut – and as long as you're not – just smile and nod in generous agreement when your mother-in-law praises the new girl. Her novelty will soon wear off – but your bitterness will increase and your attractiveness diminish if you don't come to terms with your resentment.

Another interesting slant on the sisters-in-law angle is this letter which, I felt, needed stronger advice than the hold-the-candle-to-the-devil suggestion I often make in in-law situations. . . .

Q. My husband's younger brother has always been very close to both of us. When he became engaged we were happy for him, though we were sad not to see so much of him. We met his girl friend only once before the wedding and she made it quite plain that as a local councillor's daughter, she didn't want too much to do with inferior people like us.

Since they have been married we rarely see them and when we do, it's painful. Everything we do or have, she goes one better. I hate to see my husband and his only brother drifting apart, but his snobby wife seems determined to separate them. How can I stop the drift?

A. Genuinely 'top people' are modest. They do not flaunt their position or boast about their possessions – or look down on *anybody*. Your sister-in-law is not a nice person. Still, she's in the family and because you rightly want the brothers to stay close, you must try to make her realise how offensive she is.

She might be furious with you, of course. This idiot deserves a few short sharp words – like asking her who the hell she thinks she is. But you'd better go softly for she's clearly not the type to agree that a frank confrontation could clear the air. Best to point out to her calmly and kindly the simple truth that by behaving so snobbishly, she is stressing her insecurity – not demonstrating her superiority. She may stomp off with her nose in the air and never step over your threshold again and that's a chance you've got to take. It seems to me it's a chance worth taking, for if you do nothing, the drift will continue until the break becomes final.

But mention my suggestions to your husband before you carry them out. Otherwise you might find yourself carrying the whole responsibility for an eventual separation of the brothers.

Sex frequently rears its inconvenient head within the family circle. Occasionally distressed people tell me of their sexual desire for a brother or a sister; first cousins frequently fall in love and ask if it's permissible to marry and I am able to reassure them. A widower wants to marry his dead wife's sister (it is legally possible). But quite often confessions of inter-family sexual encounters come my way too late for me to warn of possible frightful consequences, although I have published some as a warning to others who might be tempted to overstep the bounds of commonsense, if not propriety.

Q. My wife and I often make up a foursome with my brother and sister-in-law. We get on well together and the two girls have always been friends. Recently we went to a party and I'm afraid we got very drunk. During the evening my sister-in-law and I began flirting with each other. It started just as a joke, but by accident, we found an empty bedroom and then the next thing I knew, we were making love.

Now I feel terrible and though she says we should just forget it, I would like to make a clean breast of it to my brother. I feel guilty whenever I see him.

A. It's strange that you seem to feel no guilt about cheating on your wife – only on your brother. There are one or two strange things about your letter. You say you found an empty bedroom 'by accident'. What did you do – open several doors until you accidentally found one unoccupied room? And it all started, you say, as a joke. I don't believe there was anything comical or accidental in this party game you played.

I think you've been hankering after your sister-in-law and she you for longer than either will admit. Now you must face the fact that unless you practise restraint, two marriages can come unstuck.

Certainly do *not* tell your brother. The very fact that you would like to indicates you'd secretly like to admit to him that you want his wife. Think what such a confession would do: it would kill his brotherly love, splinter his marriage – or break it – ruin yours. Is this what you really want? If so, confess. If not, keep quiet and reduce the number of four-some meetings until you can resume strictly brotherly feelings for your brother's wife.

The accident of relationship, by blood or marriage, cannot clamp sexual desire. After all, the most fundamental relationships – mother/son, father/daughter – are based on sexuality. Western civilisation may have put prohibitions on familial sexuality, but the body knows no such prohibition. One of the saddest letters on this subject came from a middle-aged man.

Q. My wife and I were delighted when my son married a year ago. But a dreadful thing has happened. At forty-seven, I have fallen in love with my twenty-three-year-old daughter-in-law. She arouses every masculine instinct in me – except a paternal one. In fairness to her, she treats me like a father.

I am devoted to my wife but I cannot control my feelings for this girl. My wife has remarked on my lack of interest in love-making and I've told her it's simply my age. But it isn't. It's because I want my son's wife. I am deeply ashamed of my feelings and it has cost me a lot to write to you, but there is no one, of course, I can talk to. Is there any way you can help me?

A. There is no way anyone can help you to control your feelings for your daughter-in-law. People cannot put a rein on their emotions or their sexual desires. What you can – and must – try to control are your actions. You need to maintain the strictest self-discipline so as not to reveal your longing for her by a word or a look or a touch.

You could put your own marriage in jeopardy if you gave away your desperate secret. You would be bound to alienate your son and his wife, both of whom, I imagine, would be utterly shocked if they realised the truth.

Try to be practical, if you can. Imagine what would happen if your family became aware of the situation. Your wife might leave you. Your son would never want to see you again. You wouldn't win the girl. You'd end up alone. It's a black picture and I have to paint it starkly to warn you of the consequences of a foolish move.

I know of no way I can help you to cure yourself of this

infatuation but I hope you'll see it as an illness from which, with luck, and iron control, you will recover.

I'm glad you told your wife that reassuring white lie about your inability to make love to her. When the present sickness has passed, perhaps you'll be able to turn to her for consolation. If it helps you at all, remember that many men of your age fall for a younger woman. It's tragic that your restless urge is pinned to your son's wife. Your shame and guilt make it harder for you than if you'd fallen for a stranger. I wish I could ease your pain.

Our relatives are imposed upon us; we are thankfully free to choose our friends. It seems therefore extraordinary that we so often choose friends who cause us such pain and suffering. Over and over again people write about the meanness of friends, the jealousy of friends, their spite, their possessiveness. It would seem that the easiest thing in the world is to get rid of a friend who turns out to be more of an enemy. A simple 'please don't call or ring me again' would swiftly end the association. But sometimes it appears that it's no easier to break a friendship than a marriage.

In the case of friendships between women, opposites appear to attract. One woman is weak and dependent; her friend strong and bossy. Curious love-hate relationships survive until the hate finally becomes more powerful than the love.

Q. Three years ago, a young wife like myself and I started meeting for coffee every morning with our small children. I liked her very much. She is lively and intelligent and we soon became close friends. But she has a very strong personality and I am easy-going. More and more she is dominating my life. In fact, she bullies me about practically everything from what to feed my little boy to what clothes I should wear.

Lately, she's started telling me how to run my marriage, which is a very happy one. I know I should stand up to her, but quarrels upset me terribly. Is there any way I can tactfully tell her to mind her own business without causing an upsetting rumpus which could end our friendship?

5

A. If you continue to allow yourself to be dominated by your friend, in time you'll discover you won't be able to buy a chump chop at the supermarket without her approval. She'll probably make you get loin chops instead.

At a more serious level than chops, you certainly risk disruption of your happy marriage, if not worse. She has no mandate, as the politicians say, for running your life and you *must* assert your independence. You took on responsibilities when you married: to your husband and child, to the running of your home. No outsider has the right to undermine those responsibilities.

If you are too weak to tell your friend to leave you to run things the way you want to, you can listen politely to her orders and simply ignore them. She can't jail you for disobedience. But it would be better if you could bring yourself to tell her firmly that friendly interest in your affairs is one thing, but domineering interference is something you will not endure.

I'd like to tell you to abandon her but I doubt if you've the strength of character to do it. I warn you, though, that unless you get this friendship on a sensible balanced basis, you'll live to regret your gutless weakness.

Commonest of all letters about alleged friends are those which describe how these friends have been kind enough to arouse suspicions about a spouse's fidelity. 'My best friend whom I trust implicitly tells me she has seen my husband several times with a woman in his car. She told me for my own sake so that I could confront my husband and get the truth out of him. He says it's true. The woman is a colleague to whom he sometimes gives a lift and he swears there's nothing sinister and that he has never been unfaithful, not even in thought. But my friend thinks I'm a fool to believe him. I don't know who to listen to.'

Women who write a letter like this – and thousands do – receive a short sharp reply from me about the inadvisability of paying attention to stupid and unkind gossip.

'What motive might your best friend have?' I ask. 'Is she jealous of your husband, of your marriage? If she was a true friend, she would resist passing on malicious information. To be really friendly, she could have had a quiet and private word with your husband, warning him that transporting his colleague could be misconstrued.'

Husbands also write about 'friends' who drop hints to wives when there is absolutely no foundation for mean gossip. I suspect that countless marriages have been damaged, if not destroyed, by well-meaning – or ill-meaning-friends.

Neighbours are as mischievous as friends – even more so for friends can usually invent the justification of affection while neighbours have no such excuse for unwarranted gossip and interference.

Q. I have been happily married for twenty-seven years and worship my wife. But now my world seems to be falling apart, for I recently met, by chance, a woman who used to be a next door neighbour and who moved to another town. She hinted that our second child, a daughter aged twenty-one, is not mine, but was the result of an affair my wife had during a time when I was working away from home for fairly long periods.

My wife and the woman neighbour never got on and my wife always avoided her whenever she could. I wonder now if it was because she knew something my wife wanted to keep dark. I love my daughter, who has just made me a proud grandfather, but I am beside myself with suspicion and misery. Should I tackle my wife – and if so, how? Please help if you can.

A. Of all the mean and spiteful insinuations I've heard, this one takes the top prize. I advise you to dismiss completely from your mind the unsavoury hints this woman dropped. I'm sure she's lying, probably because your wife's offhand treatment of her when you were neighbours still rankles. I dare say the reason your wife avoided her then was because she was so unspeakable, and quite right too, except that the fiend is now trying to get her own back.

I don't think for a moment that there's a word of truth in

the allegations but if you consider it all calmly, even if it was possibly true, how could the woman know? And if she did know for sure, what kind of creature would tell a husband after all these years? No one with a grain of sense would pay the slightest attention to anything such a character says.

You worship your wife; you love your daughter. You are lucky to have two such desirable females to adore. And now a grandchild to love and spoil, too. Pray for many more years to go on loving them and try to forgive, if you can, the woman who did her best to spoil your happy life. She must be a very unhappy woman to create such wicked havoc.

It would be absurd to condemn out of hand all friends and neighbours on the grounds that there is some kind of self-interest in their advice. Here is one who performed a worthwhile friendly, neighbourly – if embarrassing – duty.

Q. I was deeply offended when a neighbour I've been very friendly with for some time asked me if I used a deodorant – and if not, said I should start to. I am a very fussy person, extremely careful about my appearance and bath every day. She's a rather envious type and I think she was just being spiteful. I should like to ignore her from now on but this isn't easy as I see her around the shops almost every day. Should I cut her dead?

A. What you should do is rush up to her next time you see her and thank her for her advice. It takes a good friend to be able to hand out such advice and a sensible woman to accept it gratefully. Even if you do use a deodorant regularly, sometimes a change of brand is a very good idea and however fussy people are, they are not always aware of offending. They're lucky to have a friend to tell them, for without such a friend, they could drive away others less kind and forthright.

I expect your neighbour thought about it for quite a while before bracing herself to mention such a sensitive subject. Be thankful to her. She's shaken your self-confidence a bit.

And she was right. There are some things we can be too self-confident about and we all at times need someone to pull us up short and make us wonder if we're quite as okay as we think we are.

'No man', said John Donne the poet, 'is an island.' But the trouble with most of us, when we try to build up and maintain relationships (or are born into them) is that we see ourselves as islands, as individuals, failing so often to understand that just as action brings reaction, so people within relationships interact with or against each other. I am forever begging people to be tolerant towards each other, to listen as well as to talk, to accept that each one of us, individual though we may feel ourselves to be, is dependent on several other individuals with whom our lives are interwoven.

It's infinitely more rewarding to be loving and giving than it is to be wanting and taking. But sadly, the lovers and givers are all too often victimised by the wanters and takers. It happens in families, with relatives, with friends, with lovers. Mutual respect of the individual, beginning with respect for the infant in the cradle, could reduce the painful problems about the difficulties of relationships which land on my desk every day.

The Sexual Misfits

'I have at last admitted to myself that I am doomed to be a homosexual. . . .' 'To my horror, I have discovered that the man I love and planned to marry is a transvestite. . . .' 'We are broken-hearted beyond telling, for our only daughter has confessed that she is a lesbian. . . .' 'My husband's sexual demands frighten me. His behaviour can only be described as bestial. . . .'

Am I normal? Can my son (or daughter) ever lead a normal life? Is my husband perverted? Is what we do together abnormal? Is it possible for a man like me to marry and lead a normal life? Is oral sex perverted? How can a man who goes with prostitutes claim to be normal? These are questions which crop up again and again.

Normal and abnormal, deviant and perverted are words which have earned a sexual connotation in a society which is based on moral, heterosexual marriage. The norm is seen as a married couple practising straight sex.

To many stolid and solid married couples, straight sex means a man and woman doing nothing beyond engaging in sexual intercourse in the 'missionary' (man face down on top of prone woman) position and any variation of this classic (sometimes known as 'English') position is regarded as being outside the norm. Outside the pale, in fact, and darkly sinister.

Most of those who consider themselves 'normal' regard any deviation, however slight, as abnormal or perverted. The couple who regularly and monotonously assume the missionary position once a week on Saturday night would be convinced that those who practise oral sex on Sunday morning are both perverted and immoral, for even in today's relatively progressive, less ignorant climate, the 'normal' are shocked by and censorious of any deviation, however minor.

It is believed that one in ten British males is homosexual: active or latent. It is impossible to estimate the number of transvestites, of seemingly perfectly ordinary 'respectable' single or married men who, under their dark neat business suits are wearing women's underclothes.

No one can guess how many couples practise buggery or act out their fetishes. No one knows how many women have lesbian relationships or how many women secretly love and desire other women.

Who can tell how many couples enjoy sado-masochism in the privacy of their bedrooms? Police records show a steady procession of paedophiliacs, exhibitionists and frotteurists. The victims though, of men who interfere with children, who expose their genitals to women, who rub their genitals against women in crowded places are frequently reluctant to make formal complaints. And it is, in any case, often very difficult for the police to track down deviant offenders.

Deviant, perverted, normal and abnormal are four of the most misused words in the sexual vocabulary and the ignorance and intolerance with which they are generally viewed creates immeasurable unhappiness and despair.

My correspondence regularly and frequently contains requests for definitions of sexual normality, both from those who suffer from fears of abnormality and engage in what they describe as abnormal practices, and those whose lives are in some way affected by those practices. But there is no clear way of defining or judging what is normal.

A sexual practice which is acceptable to one person may well be revolting to another. However, most people have their own predetermined ideas about what deviates from the socially accepted norm and what constitutes perverted practice and there is a genuinely held fine line which divides, for the majority of people, normal from the abnormal. The result of this acceptance of 'normal' above the line and 'abnormal' below it is the underlying theme, in almost all the letters I receive about deviant behaviour, of guilt and fear.

Thankfully, society is gradually becoming increasingly tolerant towards the more commonplace forms of deviant behaviour. Homosexuality, for instance, is now seen as shocking and disgraceful only by the most bigoted or the most ignorant citizens. Nevertheless, countless homosexuals still suffer immense pain and guilt; their families often feel humiliation, disappointment and shame. Some see it as a sickness, a shameful disease to be concealed. Some regard their homosexual children as pariahs. One father who wrote to me describing his twenty-year-old son as an obscene monster, said the only answer for the boy and his 'foul lover' was castration.

Homosexuals are often the victims of unspeakable cruelty and spite. How, ask near-demented parents, can their son, brought up in a decent home with decent standards of behaviour, with a loving mother and a father who never hesitated to impose discipline, turn out to be 'a bloody queer?' If such parents were told that they were perhaps responsible for their son's deviation, they would be the first, strenuously and angrily, to deny it. Yet the generally held psychiatric view is that the deviant, through some shortcoming in his childhood relationships with his parents, grows up to believe he is unlovable. He is unable to identify with the role assigned by society to the male or female.

The course of early development is directed towards achieving and discovering identity and to becoming a sexually mature adult and the progress towards this development is dependent on identity with the parent of the same sex. The boy whose father is a bully or who shows little affection or who is often absent from the home or who is disinterested in his child stands a poor chance of developing into a confident, adult male. He stands a very good chance, though, of developing into a homosexual, particularly if his mother, in an attempt to compensate him, over-reacts and smothers him with anxious maternal love.

Many cases of sexual deviation have been shown to be caused by a lack of an adequate sexual model in childhood. If a father and son have a close, loving relationship, the boy will model himself on this good male pattern. But if the father is hateful or hostile, the child will try to be as unlike his father as possible.

Almost always an over-compensating mother produces a son who grows up to regard a relationship with a woman as one of dependency – as a threat to sexuality. Which is why so many homosexuals enjoy the company of older women with whom they need not have a sexual attachment.

As boys grow older, they need to break away from the protective love of their mothers; often they turn to other men who do not seem to represent a sexual threat. Many young boys have secret crushes on older men: on teachers or sports idols or dashing heroes, for these dream heroes take the place of an inadequate father and many adolescent homosexual attachments are inspired by this kind of worship for a seemingly ideal older man.

The homosexual often idolises 'masculine' men but is unable to feel masculine himself. The homosexual who is attracted by 'softer', feminine types of male is usually seeking a substitute for a woman. But a woman, for him, poses a sexual threat; a man is a safer substitute.

Generally, homosexual relationships seem to suffer from far more tensions and difficulties than heterosexual relationships. Where a heterosexual couple will often jog along resignedly in a far from satisfactory marriage, homosexual affairs abound with problems. Jealousy is one of the greatest causes of misery, for the partners are competitive without having a clearly defined role. And because each suffers from a feeling of inferiority, they are ultra-sensitive and touchy. They are often bitchy and cruel and spiteful to each other. Their insecurity makes them over-possessive.

Most of the letters I receive from homosexuals who have adjusted to and accepted their condition write about jealousy and tensions within the relationship. Few such relationships seem to provide the partners with a secure feeling of having a lasting, tranquil relationship, although there are, indeed, some extremely happy and fulfilled homosexual couples who remain together in warmth and deep accord and love until death parts them.

Among the saddest letters I get are those from elderly, bereft homosexuals whose loneliness is beyond relief. But the majority

5*

of relationships are marred, it seems to me, by a continual search for something neither partner can find: lasting emotional security and total trust. It's often missing from heterosexual marriages; homosexuals, though, seek it even more desperately.

Despite the increased tolerance society now shows towards this particular deviation, many young homosexuals find themselves up against implacable bias and intolerance within their own family circle. Filled with doubts, shame and fear – keeping the secret of their sexual preferences to themselves – they are forced to endure parents' searching questions about why they don't bring girls home, or why they don't find a steady girl friend.

Many try to establish relationships with girls to satisfy their parents – or in the hope that a relationship with a girl will make them 'normal'. When fathers discover that their sons are 'bent', often there are terrible consequences. Boys have written to tell me their fathers whipped them, punched them, beat them up, threw them out of the house. Mothers frequently accept their sons' deviation more calmly although they express regret and disappointment.

Many boys seek reassurance from me that they are not *really* homosexuals – only temporary ones. . . .

Q. I have just had a terrible quarrel with my parents who have found out that I am a homosexual. I am seventeen years old and my friend is a teacher at the college I attend, and we have had sexual relations.

My father hit me and called me awful obscene names and has forbidden me to go on seeing this man. My parents say that if I avoid him I will become normal. Is this possible?

I feel that my parents are wrong and that I am gay but I hate to upset them, especially my mother who cried for hours after the quarrel. I am deeply depressed and worried and hope you can help me to sort myself out.

A. I wonder why you are so positively certain that you are, in fact, a committed homosexual. Your attachment to this man may simply be part of the not unusual adolescent pattern. Most people go through the stage of loving a member of the same sex. Many actually make the ultimate sexual demonstration of that love. But it does not follow that because a boy has powerful physical, as well as emotional, feelings towards another male, that he is necessarily homosexual.

The pupil-teacher relationship is a classic one, all mixed up, as it is, with hero worship. It almost always breaks up when the pupil leaves school and starts a new phase of life. And suddenly discovers that girls are lovable and desirable, too.

Your parents seem to think – and hope – this is what will happen to you. They may or may not be right. Whether or not you will continue to be convinced of your homosexuality must be guesswork. And I am not going to make any guesses.

Your father's violent reaction, your mother's sorrowful tears were to be expected. Few parents are able to face such a revelation calmly. Try to be tolerant towards them, even though they, in their ignorance, show so little of it.

Your depression is caused partly by your uncertainty about your sexual role and future, partly because you long for love and partly because you are still groping to know yourself. All of us face this kind of depression during our teens when the pain of growing up is so great.

As you mature, your future role will become clearer to you. You will learn, I hope, to accept yourself for what you are and acceptance of that role, whether homo or heterosexual, will help to banish the natural depression. Whatever the future holds, be thankful that you can give and receive love.

It is often comforting for parents to convince themselves that their homosexual sons are suffering from a sickness which, they think, can be cured by a visit to the doctor who will write out a prescription for the patient so that he'll recover in a few days. . . .

Q. I am a widow with three sons but this letter concerns my youngest who is nineteen. He admits he is a homosexual. For the last six months he has been going around with a man ten years older and when I threatened to have a word with his friend and suggested to my son that he saw the doctor, he became hysterical and sobbed like a girl. He is a good and loving son, but his blatant behaviour is breaking my heart.

A. There is nothing whatever you can do to change your son – if that's really what you're asking me, as I gather it is. But what you *can* do is help him to accept himself for what he is, by accepting him yourself for what he is: a good and loving son.

You describe his behaviour as blatant. In other words, he doesn't try to hide his homosexuality, which is better for him – and healthier – than trying to pretend he is hetero-sexual. You want him to see a doctor. Why? He isn't ill. He is not suffering from a disease – only from despair at being frustrated in his longing to love another man.

I know it is tragic from your point of view, for you cannot imagine how he can ever be happy. But you must think of him, not of yourself. He *can* be happy if those who love him respect him.

His sexual preferences are his own business. We are all entitled to enjoy sex in our own way, provided we are adult and find adult partners with whom we can be fulfilled. He became hysterical when you wanted to break up his friend-ship. Perfectly understandable. You would have reacted in the same way if someone had tried to break up your romance with his late father. I dare say you're thinking 'that's different'. Certainly it is, but love is love and third party interference, however well meaning, cannot be tolerated by lovers. If, by your attitude, you instil in him deep and lasting guilt, you'll have failed sadly in your effort to be a good mother to a good son.

Many homosexuals, in a vain endeavour to block their natural preferences, marry. They hope that marriage will somehow make them 'normal'. Most of these marriages are understandably dismal failures. Unable to endure a sexual relationship with a woman, repelled by a woman's touch and the intimacies of married life, homosexual husbands frequently engage in illicit affairs with other men.

Often the sexually frustrated and suspicious wife is convinced that her husband is seeing another woman and when she learns the truth, she is even more appalled, she says, than she would have been if another woman had been involved. Only very occasionally does a wife express relief that the third party is male. 'At least,' one wrote, 'he will continue to live with me as my official husband and no one will ever know what's going on, for he has promised me that if I can manage to close my eyes to his relationship with the man he loves (yes, he actually *loves* this man!), he will go on living in our home, and be a good husband, as far as he can be, and a good father. We shall have separate rooms, of course, and I'll have to make some plausible excuse to the children about this and about their father's occasional absences. Although I feel utterly repelled by it all, I am trying to adjust to a different and, what I know will be, a difficult life. But I still love him in a way. I still need him as a companion.'

This is an interesting example of a woman to whom married status is more important than a fulfilling marriage. And of a man who would rather maintain an outward show of domestic 'respectability' than give up the world for love. But for the majority of wives, even the faintest murmur of a husband's one-time homosexual relationship is unbearable.

Q. My world fell apart the other night when my husband was telling me about his life at boarding school. Apparently he had a serious homosexual relationship with one of the other boys and he says it was rewarding and good while it lasted. It began, he says, when they were fourteen and went on for about two years. He laughed about it and he thought I would, too. But I find it utterly sickening and it has completely put me off him physically.

We have been married seven years and have two children

and sex has always been marvellous but now I cannot bear him to touch me. I am sleeping – or trying to – on the couch downstairs. I suppose I still love him, but how can I possibly go on living with him?

A. A homosexual affair between a couple of fourteen-year-old schoolboys cannot be described as serious. You are exaggerating the importance and seriousness of it all. Schoolboys at boarding schools are obviously at risk. They are growing into adolescence and becoming sexually potent in an all-male environment. They either masturbate or have relationships with other boys. It is commonplace. And not only in boarding schools. Most children engage in physical experiments with their own sex; your own children are probably no different. It is part of the process of growing-up.

When they are able to make heterosexual relationships, they move easily into normal relationships with the opposite sex. If your husband was a latent homosexual, I imagine you would have known about it long ago. But he grew out of it, just as children grow out of other childish practices. Hopscotch and snakes and ladders, for example.

He laughed at his remembrances of things past. So should you. Laugh and then forget it. If that's all you have to worry about in your marriage, you are a very fortunate woman indeed. If you persist in this nonsensical rejection and continue to sleep on the couch and act out the drama like some latter-day Lillie Langtry, you may well drive your husband to find consolation with a more mature woman whose sense of humour and sense of proportion is healthy.

Female homosexuality is less common than the male deviation. Or so it appears. Psychiatrists say that lesbians are statistically fewer but I question their conclusion. They may indeed have fewer women patients, for women are more easily able to repress their sexual feelings than men. And the sexual needs of women may be less acute, although I question this generally held belief, too. Women may have been conditioned for centuries to repress their sexuality but this doesn't prove they have less of it than men have. A man is unable, because of the physical arrangement of his genital equipment, easily to conceal his desires; a woman's genitals are so arranged as to be more neatly tucked away out of sight but they are just as sensitive to stimulation as the male's.

Lesbian love is, in my view, as prevalent as male homosexual love. But just as she is able to conceal sexual excitement, so is she able to conceal or to repress sexual need. Many women who have close women friends with whom they live or whom they see almost every day and whom they regard simply as beloved companions are probably motivated by strong lesbian tendencies, which they do not even faintly recognise as such.

I believe that there are as many latent lesbians as there are male homosexuals, but agree with the psychiatrists that fewer women actually engage in sexual practices with members of their own sex. The majority of women – including latent lesbians – would find the idea of sexual contact with another woman unspeakably repulsive but the honest ones will admit to crushes on teachers or older girls at school and to special friendships with 'best' friends which were on a highly emotional level.

Just as boys make their fathers the principle male model for their adult development, so girls see their mothers as the principle model of femininity, although other older women will also represent an ideal of perfect womanhood. As she matures, she identifies with these ideal feminine qualities and the 'normal' heterosexual girl will finally develop into an adequate and confident woman. Having 'grown' her own femininity, she need not continue to admire it in others and other women cease to attract her. She will compete with them to attract men, use them, perhaps, to further this end but she is not drawn to them sexually.

But some girls fail to make the transition from uncertain adolescent to well-adjusted adult. They remain convinced that they are not 'properly' feminine. Sometimes they are plain and shy. They believe that men will not find them desirable. They remain adolescent in outlook even into middle and old age. They are never able to establish the femininity patterned on their mothers or on the older women they admired. They grow into lonely women seeking love and if they are lucky, they find it with another woman.

It surprises or shocks 'straight' people when I state that the lone woman who finds love with someone of her own sex is lucky, but I take the simple view that everyone who finds love is lucky for without it, life is lean and arid and hopeless. And if a woman is unable, for any reason, to achieve a 'normal' heterosexual bond, an 'abnormal' homosexual one will – if her luck holds – provide her with warmth and fulfilment.

I have been severely criticised by 'straight' people for what they describe as my permissive attitudes towards 'gay' people but the critics usually speak from a position of smug righteousness; their lives are neither lonely nor loveless. It's easy enough to condemn from a stance of security but from where I sit, at the receiving end of so much despair, I take the view that any kind of love, any warm companionship must be grasped with gratitude.

The physical relationship between women can be as satisfying to them as a heterosexual one can be to 'normal' people. Some believe it is more satisfying, for many men fail to understand the sexual needs of women, believing that orgasm is always vaginal, not realising the importance of clitoral stimulation. Indeed several lesbians have told me that only a woman can really understand the physical needs of another woman, which while being a foolish generalised claim, makes some sense in the light of the sexual ignorance or selfishness of so many men. But some lesbians say that they are disappointed that their partners are unable to take on a more masculine role and enter them.

These are the women who seek in their partners a substitute male; in other lesbian relationships, women seek only love and physical release with each other and are frequently hostile towards men. But there is a strong bond between lesbian women and homosexual males and there are several mixed clubs and groups where 'gays' of both sexes mingle socially, bound together, perhaps, as persecuted minorities so often are, for protection against a hostile intolerant society.

Many of the letters I receive from lesbians come from married women whose husbands have left them for other women. Lonely and inconsolable, they meet a friend – another woman who is tender and kind. The deserted wife, hungry for sex and reassurance, begins to depend more and more on her friend for comfort and the inevitable happens. Whereupon the frightened wife, believing herself to be an unnatural creature, writes for 'permission' to carry on with the affair. She feels guilty, often sees the relationship as unclean and sordid and seeks reassurance from me that it is neither of these things. And gets it.

There are so many cases of this sort that I am bound to wonder if the marriage failed because the wife was latently homosexual long before the marriage took place; or because the marriage was doomed for some other reason. Whatever the cause, it is interesting that so many women find consolation, quite soon after the break up, with another woman instead of trying to find another man. Many of the deserted wives have children and are immensely concerned about the effect on them of a lesbian love affair. . . .

Q. A year ago my husband left me for another woman. I have two small children and I have devoted myself to them, but I have been very lonely. A few months ago I met a marvellous woman and a deep relationship has grown between us. I have become aware of feelings I never knew I possessed and though I loved my husband, it was nothing like the warm rewarding and sexual love I feel for my friend. I hope this doesn't shock you.

Now my friend, who is very fond of my children and has a good job, would like us to move into her house with her. The children like her but though I know my friend and I would be happy, one worry persists. Do you think our relationship could harm the children?

A. Whether or not your homosexual relationship would harm your children depends, I think, entirely upon the way you and your friend conduct your lives. Obviously, the ideal upbringing for children is with a loving mother and father who provide them with a stable background and the right balance between opposite sexes. But your children were denied this background when their father left you. For them, therefore, any chance to grow up in a home where there is love and stability is desirable.

If you turn down the chance to live with your friend, the children will continue to lead an unbalanced life with one lonely parent. But by moving in with her, they will at any rate have two happy people caring for them and concerned about their development and future. But your relationship could damage them emotionally if they were to become aware that it was sexually based before they are old enough to understand it. In plain words, be sure they don't find you two women making love to each other. It wouldn't be wise to share a bedroom.

Be immensely discreet when they're around. You can show affection for each other, as many heterosexual women friends do – but be careful to keep the relationship at an apparent low key in the children's presence, however high the key may be when you are alone with each other. And, for the record, your revelation doesn't shock me. I do not find homosexual relationships the least bit shocking – and I hope yours brings happiness and gives you and your children the love and security you all need.

It is curious that the discovery of a lesbian daughter doesn't seem to produce the same violent reaction in parents as does the discovery of a homosexual son. I have rarely heard of a father – or mother – beating up a lesbian child, nor turning her out of the home. Letters from a girl's parents are almost always more in sorrow than in anger. . . .

Q. It was a terrible grief to me and my husband when we discovered our daughter is a lesbian. She is twenty-two and has always been reserved and aloof – and very lonely. One night, I heard her crying in her room and that was when she told me the truth. Neither of us understand her or people like her, but we want to help her for we love her.

She says she has no friend now, although she did have a relationship which ended some months ago, which is why she is so unhappy at present. What can we do for our girl, please?

A. You can treat her like you'd treat any child you cherish who is unhappy over the loss of a lover. You can be tender and kind and natural towards her. I know it's not easy for you to behave naturally, for as you say, neither you nor her father have encountered this situation before. But try to see it this way: until you discovered your daughter's homosexuality, you treated her as any parents treat their beloved children. You were probably uneasy and worried because she was a withdrawn girl and anxious for her to have friends and fun. I dare say you both discussed her solitary way of life and hoped she'd find someone to love in time. Well, poor lamb, she did. It just happened to be another woman. Had it been a man, you'd have shown great compassion for her loss. Show it now, but don't hover about her as if she were an invalid. Try, difficult as it is, to accept her for what she is – for she is now as she was before your discovery.

The sadness for you, perhaps, is the knowledge that she will not provide you with a son-in-law and grandchildren. But the most important thing is for you to recognise the need for her particular kind of love – to tell her you welcome her friends, whoever they are, in your home, to be loyal and loving to her – and not make a great outward demonstration of pity. I hope she finds love again and that you and her father can face up to her problems – as well as to your own.

There is undoubtedly a need for much wider education about homosexuality – both male and female. For while sex education has generally broadened, there seems to be a conspiracy of silence about deviations which produce dangerous myths and perpetuate the cruelties 'normal' people unwittingly (or wittingly) practise against 'abnormals'. This letter from a schoolgirl illustrates the need for sensible information. . . .

Q. There is a small group of girls in our class at school who are what my friend and I think are called lesbians. They try to lead other girls on and they write suggestive letters and pass them around in class. We are mostly aged thirteen and fourteen. My friend and I do not want to get mixed up in this horrible sort of thing and wondered if we ought to tell one of the teachers or what we should do.

A. Try not to be upset or disturbed by this group of girls. Probably almost every school has some girls who behave as they do. I doubt if they are really lesbians – I expect it's just a stage lots of adolescent people go through. It's really only experimental sex and as they mature, they'll very likely get interested in boys and lose their interest in each other and in other girls.

There is no reason why you and your friend should get involved. As for telling one of your teachers – there's no need to bother. I'm pretty sure the teachers are well aware of this sort of thing when it happens – and know that it's wise to take no notice. But there's one thing you and your friend should understand: if these girls do not develop as hetero-sexuals (which means enjoying adult relationships with the opposite sex), if they continue throughout their lives to be lesbians, they should not be objects of contempt or derision. Because they are different does not mean they are horrible, or monsters and it would be extremely cruel to scorn them or show disgust.

Most lesbians prefer not to be pitied, either. They simply want to be left alone and unharried so that they can live the sort of lives which bring them peace and contentment. They want – and are entitled to expect – to be treated like any other citizens whose sexual lives and practices are their own private affair.

I have concentrated particularly in this chapter about deviations on homosexuality and lesbianism because the letters I receive about deviations are mainly concerned with these two aspects. The nearest runner-up is transvestism. Most people believe that a transvestite who is able to perform sexually only when wearing women's garments is a homosexual. But in fact many transvestites are satisfactory lovers of women, as long as they are able to use women's clothes to stimulate their desires. The trouble comes when, fearing ridicule or disgust, they try to repress their fetish, thus repressing their sexuality.

Some transvestites, however, want to be complete women, beg for help in getting sex-change operations or, failing to achieve this very difficult objective, wear wigs and women's clothes all the time, living as far as they possibly can the outward life of a female.

Most of the problem letters about transvestism come from men who fall in love and want to marry or to have a sexual relationship. 'How will she react,' they say, 'when she finds out? Should I confess immediately? Should I marry and then tell her?' Some do just that and the result is usually disastrous, as distraught, shocked wives write and tell me.

I naturally advise transvestites to explain their sexual needs before marriage, for I know that the discovery afterwards almost always destroys the marriage. And I am very glad when girls write, as this one did when she found the man she loved was a transvestite, for they can be helped to come to terms with something which doesn't seem quite so appalling when it is explained to them.

Q. I have made a terrifying discovery about the man I love and was planning to marry. He is a transvestite. He confessed last week that for some years he has worn women's underwear and that sometimes he locks himself up in his room and wears dresses and even a long wig. He swears he is not a homosexual and says he has normal sexual desires, which I know to be true because we have made love very successfully. I am very worried and do not know what to do, for I really love him and want to marry him.

A. Transvestism is not as uncommon as you may think. It is quite true that men like your lover are not necessarily homosexuals. Many are happily married. BUT – and it's a big but – the wives play an enormously important part in maintaining a happy relationship.

Most people need sexual stimulation. Transvestism is an extreme sort of stimulation. A woman who truly loves a man can help him – by understanding and by participating. I know of very happy marriages where wives actually shop for women's clothes for their husbands and encourage them to wear them in the privacy of the bedroom. They make jokes about it all, seeing it as part of the fun of love-making, though it's not, perhaps, everyone's idea of a jolly game.

I advise you to marry only if you feel you can participate. What two people do in private is their own affair – just so long as no one is hurt or damaged or degraded. But don't think that marriage will change him into what you think of as normal.

Transvestism is an extreme form of fetishism, but there are many other less extreme forms which frighten women when they discover that the men in their lives need them for sexual stimulation. It is extremely difficult for most women to understand fetishism, for women are not fetishists. It is an entirely male deviation – or, as I prefer to call it, need.

The simple definition of a fetishist is a man who requires to substitute an inanimate object or particular part of the body for a sexual partner. A fetish may be jewellery, clothing or even a voice. Obscene telephone callers are often voice fetishists; as soon as they hear a frightened female response at the other end of the line, they are able to achieve an erection and usually masturbate.

Fetishists tend to be introverted with a rich fantasy life, sexually inadequate, guilty and anxious in any sexual situation. They fear impotence. By avoiding actual intercourse, by finding a substitute which will not reveal his hidden fears, the fetishist is able to feel more secure. Some manage intercourse by getting their wives and girl friends to wear or use the item on which they depend for stimulus: high heeled shoes, boots, black tights, small pinafores, rubber garments – the list is long and varied.

A large majority of men, while not realising it, are minor fetishists, stimulated by making love to a woman wearing some fabric which excites them, like satin or chiffon or lace. It's only when the fetish seems bizarre that women become afraid and seek help. And, as in all cases of deviation, the only help to be given is in an explanation of why a man needs to do the things which frighten her.

A surprising number of women are able to come to terms with a deviation which is explained to them. Saddest of all the fetishist letters I receive come from anonymous men who write long letters about their particular fetish needs. There was one who wrote regularly about rubber garments, pages and pages describing them and his pleasurable dreams of women wearing them. He had never been able to act out his fantasies. 'A prostitute would wear them, I suppose,' he wrote, 'but I would never have the courage to go to one.' His letters ceased about a year ago. I often wonder what became of him.

Two other main deviations which deeply concern women (they do not appear to worry many men), are sado-masochism and what they describe as unnatural or perverted sexual practices, meaning buggery.

Q. A few weeks ago we were making love and my husband started to slap me and became intensely excited when I slapped him back. Since then we have been wrestling – it sounds ridiculous I know – as part of our love play. The other evening during a particularly strenuous bout, he grabbed my hairbrush and slapped me across the buttocks. It wasn't very hard, but enough to sting. I was shocked but then he asked me to do the same to him.

I love my husband deeply and like to please him, so I did, but I must admit I was very upset by it. Is this a disgusting perversion that should be stopped?

I explained to this wife that many people are sexually excited to a greater or lesser degree by the idea of beating and sub-mission, for love and pain – or rather passion and pain – are closely associated. It certainly counts, I told her, as a deviation or perversion when it is isolated as a source of satisfaction away from actual intercourse and when there is no loving relation-ship – only brutality for the purpose of individual satisfaction.

To reassure her, I pointed out that many couples engage in harmless sado-masochistic rituals before intercourse, both of them enjoying the giving and taking of punishment. I also explained, as I do in every case where a deviation could create revulsion or undue pain or unacceptable humiliation, that no woman is bound to participate in or accept any sexual practice which she finds unendurable, for the law protects her. The commonest enquiry about legality concerns anal intercourse....

Q. This isn't really a problem, more a question. Is it illegal for a husband and wife to make love when the husband uses his wife's back passage instead of her vagina? My husband and I both get a lot of pleasure from using this kind of sexual technique, but I can't help worrying about what we do, for a friend has told me it is a punishable offence. Will you please tell me what the law is?

A. It is felony for a person to practise anal intercourse with another person (or with an animal), according to the Sexual Offences Act of 1956 and the punishment to which an offen-der is liable is life imprisonment. Between a man and a woman, each may be equally liable even when the couple are husband and wife and when each consents to the act.

Measuring Up

Only once have I actually been addressed in a letter as Dear Dr Proops, but an incredibly large number of people appear to regard me as a substitute for a doctor. Worried by various physical disabilities or by mysterious symptoms, they ask me for cures and remedies instead of going to see their GP, fearing, it seems, a snub if their complaint might appear to him to be trivial.

Impatience or lack of interest or pressure of work on the part of doctors makes people very reluctant to seek help from them. Many people tell me they are too embarrassed to ask doctors about physical impediments but they do not hesitate to ask me, for it is so much less embarrassing to describe intimate matters in a letter to a stranger than to face a doctor across a desk.

People have told me that they plucked up courage to see a doctor, carefully rehearsed, on the way to the surgery, the words in which to describe the intimate nature of the complaint, only to come up against blank disinterest and lack of sympathy or even of the basic understanding of the hot discomfiture behind the patient's halting words.

On one occasion when I had advised a woman to see her doctor about a personal problem, I received an offensive letter from the doctor's infuriated wife (who sent a copy of the letter to the *Lancet* asking the editor to publish it). She asked how I, a mere journalist, dared to waste a busy doctor's time with this woman's trivial problem. In my reply to her (I also sent a copy to the *Lancet* with a request to the editor to publish it), I pointed out that every problem which besets people and causes them anxiety should be taken seriously, that if more doctors ceased to regard such problems as trivial, they'd have fewer deeply neurotic patients in their waiting rooms and in hospitals.

The two letters, published in the *Lancet*'s Peripatetic Column, started a controversial correspondence in that magazine and, I gathered, stimulated important dialogue. Many doctors wrote to me privately expressing thanks, saying they needed reminding that their functions didn't stop at prescribing cough cures. Just the same, the volume of letters from people who *should* go to the doctor instead of asking me for help never diminishes. And perhaps it is too embarrassing for a man deeply worried about the size of his penis to ask his doctor if it means he will never be able to satisfy a woman. But he can ask me, and it is commonplace to receive letters like the following. . . .

Q. I have never had a steady girl friend or attempted to have sex for two reasons. One, I am terribly shy with girls and never know what to say to them. Two, I am very worried about the small size of my sexual organs and do not think I could satisfy a woman. I am nearly twenty-one and feel desperately miserable and depressed and inferior. Can you help me in any way?

A. Let's deal with the second problem right away, for it immensely influences the first one. The size of a man's genitals has nothing whatever to do with his virility or ability to be a satisfactory lover. Some people have small noses. They are just as useful for the job required of them as large ones. Likewise feet. A man with small feet is capable of walking for miles.

It's a myth that a man who is small in the more intimate parts is less capable of giving sexual satisfaction than men better endowed. The female vagina can accommodate every size of erect penis. Please accept this fact without question – and having accepted it (not only from me, but from medical experts), I think your shyness with girls will begin to evaporate. You are shy because you feel inadequate, convinced you'll fail them at the moment of truth. Once you begin to take my word for it that your fears are unfounded, you will begin to be confident and that's the start of feeling easy in the company of girls. And one of these days you'll find you get along so well with one particular girl that everything else will follow naturally.

One last word: there's no such thing as an inferior person. You are just one who happens, quite falsely, to think of yourself as such. Many men with very adequate and large sexual organs are inadequate as people.

While many men worry unnecessarily about a small penis, women become frantic with worry about the size of their breasts, often convinced that their small breasts make them undesirable to men or that their marriages are threatened because of their puny measurements.

Since breasts are so closely related to sexuality, not only because they are sensual zones, but because they are a powerful sexual symbol, women who are not well-endowed suffer from the same sense of inferiority and inadequacy that beset men with small genitals.

Advertising campaigns, pin-up pictures in newspapers and girlie magazines, concentrate on breast-power. The big-breasted girl is promoted as the sexually desirable girl, the girl who will attract men. Women fearful of not measuring up are actually prepared to spend their life savings on silicone injections and re-building plastic surgery because they are afraid of falling behind in sexual competition. Pleas from women for information and advice about cosmetic breast surgery have increased enormously in recent years and until women cease to be commercially promoted as big-breasted sex symbols whose bodies are designed for the pleasure of men, the letters, I prophesy, will continue to pour in.

When women tell me their husbands have ceased to love them because their breasts are undersized, I try to convince them that a faltering marriage is not going to be improved if the wife gets another couple of inches added to her bust. If the husband is straying there are certain to be other reasons. I doubt, though, if they believe me and this doubt is strengthened by men who write to say their wives are obsessed about the size of their breasts and will I please write back to say not all men are interested in huge mammary glands, so that they can convince their wives that their anxieties are groundless.

Q. I am very slightly built with a tiny bust and although it's never worried me before, I am now beginning to feel unhappy about it. I got married six months ago and I know my husband loves me. Our sex life is good in every way for I am responsive and, he says, imaginative. But he sometimes makes little remarks, jokes really, about my small breasts. When he sees I'm upset, he insists he's only teasing me. But I have seen him looking with great interest at pictures of girls with big breasts and I am fearful that he might begin to find me uninteresting to make love to.

I would gladly have plastic surgery to enlarge my breasts if you think it would be sensible. If so, could you please tell me how much it would cost and send me the name of a surgeon.

A. I am dead against the kind of teasing which masks hurtful references to any kind of physical drawback. I once knew a girl who had a funny little tip-tilted nose which was apt to twitch when she got excited. Her boy friend used to call her Rabbit-face. In public as well as in private. No one was more surprised and aggrieved than he was when she left him for a man who thought her nose enchanting.

But I am sure your husband doesn't mean to be hurtful. He is thoughtless and foolish and should know better and you can tell him I said so. Remind him that big busty girls may look sensuous and luscious, but their looks often belie their performance. A lithe, athletic, imaginative girl is a lot more fun in bed than a heavy lump. But don't just tell him. Continue to keep him aware of the fact that undersized you may be, but skilful at using what you have to great advantage, you are.

It would cost you a good deal of money – probably four to five hundred pounds – to have surgery and in my view, it would be money wasted. Even if you did decide to add a few inches, I couldn't give you the name of a surgeon. I wouldn't be allowed to. You would need to go to your family doctor first to get a letter of referral to a plastic surgeon.

Many people think they can go shopping for a new pair of breasts or a new nose or a face-lift as easily as they can pick a packet of detergent off a supermarket shelf and I have to explain over and over again that it isn't all that simple. But the requests for a new look continue to pour in and there is, in fact, a very wide range of cosmetic surgery available to those with the money and the time for such indulgences. In fact it is possible to have practically any part of the anatomy tailored to suit its owner. In Japan, they actually make girls into virgins again.

Forehead lines can be removed. Eyes can be dewrinkled. Cheeks can be lifted and padded. Nose lines can be filled and the nose straightened or reshaped. Ears can be pinned back. Mouth lines can be filled. Chins may be extended and jowls reduced. Necks may be smoothed and fleshy arms reduced. Breasts can be enlarged or reduced and moles or birthmarks removed. Stomachs can be tucked in and bottoms taken up. Knees can be dewrinkled and even feet can be reduced in size. Unfortunately though, once surgery has been performed, the patient has to return at intervals to keep the bit of the body in question tucked up or taken in.

In certain cases, people who allow their dislike of their double chin or baggy eyes to turn into a real phobia which is going to destroy their mental stability can have surgery on the National Health. But it has to be an extreme situation before free treatment is given.

Although I am in principle against drastic cosmetic surgery, I believe that an ageing woman whose wrinkles are causing her deep distress can profit by face-lifting or wrinkle removing. If she feels happier and more confident as a result of surgery which makes her look younger, she will feel better able to face her problems. But I do not believe that the surgeon's knife is the magic wand which makes bad marriages good again, or revives love which has faded.

Many young girls suffer agonies of misery about the size of their noses and a new one can boost morale. But I feel bound to point out to these unhappy girls that a nice new nose alone won't necessarily get them the handsome man of their dreams, though it will give them greater confidence in their search for him. The girl with a long or bumpy nose, obsessed by her appearance to the exclusion of all other interests, is likely to blossom with a new one.

Ideally, it would be splendid to be able to convince people worried about their appearance that personality and charm count for more than looks.

Q. I have often wondered how women of around my age (mid forties), whom I see on TV manage to keep such smooth skins. What happens to all their wrinkles? Perhaps they have face-lifts. I do wish I knew their secret, for I am a widow and I'd love to banish the crow's feet and acquire a youthful bloom and maybe a nice man to take my mind off the advancing years. You often go on TV. Have you learned the secret?

A. I haven't actually learned any secrets from TV ladies, but I do know that the make-up girls are very good at camouflaging wrinkles and other little blemishes like heavy bags under the eyes. Their handiwork, though, while absolutely right for the studio lights and cameras, wouldn't be so effective in the cold light of day. As well I know, for I've sometimes left the studio with make-up still on hoping I looked like I'd shed a few years and have had some very curious stares from passers-by.

I have come to the conclusion that a few wrinkles and a crow's foot or two are neither here nor there. Especially if the wrinkles are the result of hearty laughter. My advice to you is to treat yourself to a good night cream and a moisturising cream for daytime and stop worrying, for it's worrying about them which produces yet more wrinkles. I'm sure that when you meet a nice man, he won't be looking out for your crow's feet. He'll know that a cheerful, amiable widow with a nice sense of humour has acquired, along with the wrinkles, the real secret of life: which is how to make another human being glad to be alive.

The wearing of glasses used to be as worrying a problem for the short-sighted as small breasts are now to the meagrely endowed. Few girls care any longer about having to wear specs. For those who do, I suggest saving up for contact lenses, but I remind girls that many beautiful top models with perfect sight wear huge, eye-stopping frames with plain glass lenses because they make them look even more stunning.

In the last resort, I describe myself: always plain and rangy, short-sighted since the age of nine, buck-toothed and long nosed. Not a pretty picture. Yet despite my lack of beauty, I remind my correspondents, I had my fair share of male ad-mirers, I married, and stayed married, have been lucky enough to be loved, to lead an interesting life and do an interesting job. The secret, I tell them, is to make the best of what you've got, for you're bound to find some little bit of you that's not entirely hideous. And the rest you can learn to laugh at.

Just as undue commercial breast emphasis has encouraged complexes about small breasts, so the multi-million pound slimming aids industry has helped to create problems for plumpish women who, a few years ago, would have been regarded as comfortably and charmingly rounded. Many women believe their weight has a direct bearing on their social success or failure and on their ability to keep men happy and I get a great many letters from women convinced that because they cannot squeeze into a size 14, they are grossly overweight.

More women are probably obsessed about weight than about any other physical attribute or impediment. It's curious that while most women diet to be trim for men, many men are totally indifferent to extra pounds gained. They rarely seem to notice if their wives or girl friends have put on a stone or lost it. What they do notice is the way she picks at food, is forever talking about her diet, loses her sparkle because she thinks of little besides her weight, stops laughing or stops being loving. Indeed I know of several cases where obsessed weight-watching

wives have driven their husbands into the arms of plump jolly
women more concerned with loving than with slimming.

Many women who slim fanatically pay no attention to what
their husbands really want them to look like, only what they
assume men want. A man may tell his wife appreciatively that
she is cuddly and cosy but rarely will she believe him.

Extremely worrying to many health experts is the way very
young girls have developed slimming crazes. Their mothers
worry, too, and I receive an increasing number of letters like
this one. . . .

Q. I am so worried about my sixteen-year-old daughter. Like
all the girls in her class, she is slimming crazy. She was a bit
plump but now she looks positively scrawny. She won't stop
dieting and refuses proper meals. If I put nourishing food in
front of her she just picks at it. I wouldn't mind so much if
she wasn't so miserable. She's lost all her old bounce and I'm
sure she's making herself ill. I offer her the nice food and the
tasty puddings she used to like to tempt her, but she shouts
and leaves the table if I press her to eat. A word from you
might make her see how dangerous dieting can be. She won't
believe me.

A. Most teenage girls want to shed their puppy-fat and
change from little roly-polys into sleek young women. But
I agree with you that some girls take the slimming craze too
far, to the serious detriment of their health. You yourself,
though, could inadvertently be contributing to her problem.
You say you put tasty food and tempting puddings before
her, hoping to lure her from her diet. You would be doing her
a better service if you planned the kind of low-calorie meals
which would be nourishing without being fattening.

I advise you to get a sensible diet sheet and discuss it with
your daughter, telling her you are on her side and want to
help her to stay slim. If your doctor is a sympathetic one, he
will recommend a suitable diet for her. Fresh fruit, salads,
and vegetables and simple meals will tempt her much more

than the stodgy puddings she loved before she became figure-conscious. And they're much better, too, for her skin and overall health.

Tell her that near starvation will damage her health and destroy her looks. And if you think it will help, *do* say I said so.

A good dose of confidence-booster is all that is needed for many of the people who write seeking help for what they consider to be their physical inadequacies. However, there are a great many people who need to be persuaded to seek help for their physical problems from a GP. Often this is no easy task, for they would not have written to me in the first place if they felt able to consult a doctor about what is troubling them.

One of the most worrying and frequent problems people write to me about instead of seeking the medical attention they need, is VD. Each year over 200 million of the world's population will probably get gonorrhoea and 50 million will get syphilis. Gonorrhoea is second to measles as the world's most common infectious disease. The more permissive attitude to sex, the use of the contraceptive pill and freedom of travel have all been blamed for what is virtually an epidemic.

One of the major difficulties in stamping out VD is the stigma which is attached to the infection. Victims are afraid to report symptoms, afraid even to admit to themselves – let alone anyone else – that they might have contracted a sexually transmitted disease.

An enormous amount of ignorance and many myths surround it; widespread sexual irresponsibility spreads it. Because they are afraid of moral judgements, countless people put off a visit to a doctor or clinic which, if paid as soon as the gonorrhoea symptoms first appeared, would result in swift and effective treatment. But the young man who discovers a small ulcer on his genitals tells himself that if he ignores it, it's bound to go away. He has already deluded himself that earlier symptoms – the burning feeling when he urinates, the creamy discharge, discomfort in the urethra – are nothing to worry about. Meanwhile, the chances are that he has infected a girl friend in these early days, or several if he is as promiscuous as many young people are.

It isn't until he finally admits that the worrying symptoms won't go away if he ignores them that he writes to me, describing them. I write back immediately, begging him to see a doctor or to go at once to a clinic. I tell him where to find a clinic. I reassure him by explaining that a few weeks' simple treatment will clear the trouble but that if he neglects to get treatment or delays it, he could face extremely serious consequences.

It's easier to persuade men to seek medical help in time – for them symptoms are apparent early on. With women, though, the problem is extremely difficult, for unless they know they may have been infected, they remain unaware for some time.

The slower progress of gonorrhoea is hard to detect in females. But many write when they suffer excessive menstrual pain, are feverish and very headachy or when they feel unusual pain during intercourse or notice a painful swelling of the vulva. Letters like this get a swift answer. 'Go at once to your doctor,' I write. 'Or to any hospital, for you may well have contracted VD and you must get medical treatment.'

The trouble with so many of the people, of both sexes, who describe symptoms which are probably of gonorrhoea is that they begin their letters by saying, 'Please don't tell me to see my doctor . . .' Many people tell me they're afraid to be seen going into a clinic for everyone will know why they're going there. I point out that fears about going to a doctor or clinic are nothing to the fears they will face if they fail to take immediate action.

People of all ages ask about how it's contracted: 'Can I get VD by sitting on a public lavatory seat?' 'Could the sore on my mouth be VD? I drank out of a cracked cup at a cafe but I've never been with anyone but my husband.' 'Can you get VD by kissing someone even if you don't have sex with them?' 'Could a boy give it to me by touching my private parts?' 'Is it true that VD can be passed from a mother to her unborn child?'

I explain that venereal diseases are sexually transmitted, that oral sex can cause infection, that unborn babies can be infected by the mother, that lavatory seats and cracked cups are not sources but that hygiene is immensely important whether a person is at risk of VD or not.

Answering letters about VD are the only occasions when I deliberately set out to frighten people into seeking urgent medical help, spelling out the consequences of failure to do so in the plainest possible terms.

This letter from a fifteen-year-old girl expresses fear, not only of going to a doctor, but of her parents, too. . . .

Q. In the past few months I have been having sex with three boys and I think that I have got VD. I have got a sore place and it hurts when I go to the loo. I am too scared to tell my parents as I am not yet sixteen and I'm very worried about going to the doctor in case he tells them for they would go mad. He would also tell me off because he has known me since I was young. If I went to see him, am I old enough for him not to inform my parents, and if not, where can I go so that I can be really sure they won't tell them?

A. If you are old enough to get VD you are certainly old enough to take yourself to a doctor and get him to examine you. He is not under any *legal* obligation to keep your secret from your parents, but he shouldn't tell – not if he feels ethically bound by the oath he takes when he qualifies. But some doctors believe (wrongly in my view) that parents ought to know when their children get into this kind of situation.

If you want to be absolutely certain of secrecy, there are special VD clinics you can go to – usually attached to a hospital. Most big hospitals have them. It's against the law for the clinics to divulge information to anyone about their patients – whatever their age.

Don't waste any more time worrying. Get moving and get rid of it. You shouldn't be worrying about your parents finding out. You should be worrying about the dangerously nasty pay-off promiscuity can lead to.

An extraordinary number of teenagers are under the impression that adolescent acne is a sign that they may have VD. Acne causes more youthful teenage anguish than almost any other physical condition. Girls tell me they won't go out, won't even, in extreme cases, go to school and roam the streets playing truant rather than face other girls and boys in the classroom. They become frantic as holiday times approach and they will have to expose spotty backs on beaches.

Girls and boys ask for cures, for disguising cover-ups, for names of magical ointments, and are convinced their burgeoning pimples will destroy their lives forever. One fourteen-year-old girl had heard of skin-peeling beauty treatment, had saved up £6 out of her pocket money and wanted to be recommended to a beautician to have her acne peeled off.

It isn't easy to convince teenagers that the loathsome spots which are ruining their lives will, like puppy-fat, disappear in the fullness of time if they're careful about the food they eat and if they take proper care of themselves. 'Don't just sit about hunched over the telly night after night,' I tell them – always writing in a fairly light-hearted vein without dramatics. 'Get off your rear end and take some exercise in the freshest air you can find. A park, for instance. Go jogging with another girl – or another boy – and stir your lazy circulation. Wash your spotty skin with a medicated soap you can buy at the chemists. Always be meticulous about using clean face cloths and towels. Wash your hair as often as you can, with a medicated shampoo. It won't hurt to wash it every day. Scrub your back with a loofah or brush. Keep your hands and nails clean and try not to scratch. Never squeeze spots. Drink pints and pints of cold water instead of all that pink bottled stuff. Cut out sweets, chocolates, cakes, puddings and greasy food. Don't have chips with everything. Salads and fruit and green vegetables are good for you. So are eggs and fish, chicken and meat in moderation.

'There's no need to starve, in fact it's dangerous to starve and it won't make the spots go away. But go away they positively will if you're sensible. They won't vanish overnight or even in a week and you'll have to be patient and not get fed up and stop trying just because you don't see an immediate, magic improvement. Take my word for it that if you follow my advice it'll begin to dawn on you that your skin's getting better and better. And when you look around and see older girls and boys with nice, clear complexions, you'll realise that they suffered once, just as you do now. Practically everyone does. And hardly anyone has them in their later teens – only those who haven't bothered to try to cure them.'

Cancer is still a taboo word and when women write, as thousands do, about their fears of cancer, they avoid the use of the word in expressing their terror of it.

Countless women who discover lumps on their breasts write to me, afraid not only of getting confirmation of their worst fears from their doctors, but afraid even to submit themselves for examination. Some women are afraid to examine their own breasts, or 'don't like', they say, to touch themselves – a hang-up, perhaps, from a mother's exhortation to a child not to mess about with her body on the grounds that it's 'not nice' to touch yourself.

As with all other medical enquiries, I plead with women to see their doctors immediately, reassuring them that a lump on the breast does not necessarily mean what they dread – and even if it did, prompt action can often halt the spread of the growth. Many women have written back to say they were thankful they finally plucked up courage, that the lump was successfully removed with no complications.

Q. I am so scared, in fact I am petrified. Last week I discovered a lump on my breast and I am too terrified of doctors and hospitals to find out what's wrong. I can't sleep with the worry of it and I feel I am going out of my mind. Please, please help me.

A. I have been worried, too, ever since your letter arrived – worried because I would like you not to waste another second or have one more sleepless night over something that could easily prove to be very trivial indeed. You are scared of doctors and hospitals. Lots of people are, quite needlessly.

Doctors and hospitals are there to help, to discover what's wrong and set about putting it right. They are dedicated to making people well.

You haven't mentioned the dreaded word cancer, so I will. That's what you're really scared of, isn't it? But the lump could so easily be a harmless little cyst. Whatever it is, you must brace yourself to see a doctor and the sooner you do it, the better for your peace of mind and your health.

'Please, please help,' you said to me. The best help I can possibly give you is to beg you to seek it professionally and I hope you'll write to me again soon telling me all your fears were totally unfounded.

But sometimes a woman has to be told a mastectomy is required and the letters from those who have had a breast removed are pitiful. Curiously, many such women are even more terrified of what the operation will do to their marriage than they are of the medical prognosis.

Q. I have had eighteen years of wonderful marriage. We are very happy and make love regularly. Now I am sure all this will stop. My doctor has told me I must have a breast removed. He tried to reassure me but it didn't help. Although I am, of course, very worried about the operation, I am even more worried about my marriage. I feel as if I will no longer be a woman and I am so afraid my husband will be repelled.

I haven't told him yet. Somehow I cannot bear to, for he will be so distressed. How can a man want to go on living with someone so maimed? What can I do, Marje? I love him so much. I am beside myself with worry.

A. It is no wonder you have such a happy marriage and loving husband, for you are brave and incredibly unselfish. You are thinking of him more than of yourself. But look at it this way: if the doctor had told your husband that he needed an operation which would make him impotent, what would be your reaction? Suppose his testicles had to be removed –

would you love him less? Would you shudder away from the
prospect of physical contact with him? Of course not. You
would be overwhelmed with the urge to help him and
cherish him and console him. And that is exactly how he will
react when you break your news to him.

His first thought will be for you, for your swift recovery
and your return home to his arms. That's what real love is all
about, as you will discover. As for sex, this operation will
make not the slightest difference once you're through the
convalescent period. I know many women – some very
young ones – who've had it done and they are as attractive,
as feminine and as sexually fulfilled as they were before the
operation. I am not just saying all this to reassure you. It's
true. As, in time, you will discover for yourself.

It is essential to give every possible reassurance to women
who have to face a mastectomy, for more than any other kind of
operation, it scars her, not only physically but fundamentally.
Her body is flawed; her femininity is threatened. Women equate
their desirability with their looks and the woman whose breast
is removed feels that her womanhood is taken from her.

I am thankful that I know a photographic model, now in her
early thirties, who had a mastectomy a few years ago. I am thus
able to tell distraught women that the scar is by no means the
searing wound they fear (I've seen it and it's neat and her breast
is white and smooth). I can also tell them that this young
woman actually models skinny sweaters – with the use of a
good bra – that her beauty is unimpaired, that her love life is the
envy of many of her friends.

There have been enormous advances in the after-care of
breast surgery patients, as well as in the operation techniques.
And the beautifully designed bras now available make it
possible for women to face the world without embarrassment.

Women often write telling me they have heard that cervical
tests can detect early cancer symptoms. Women who go to
clinics for contraceptive advice are given a test automatically.
But it rarely occurs to those who are not having regular check-
ups to get their doctors to arrange a smear test. Older women,

particularly, are reluctant to be 'messed about with', and refuse to be examined.

Whenever there's even a faint chance that a few words from me might encourage them to go to a health clinic or doctor, I write about neglect which can cause so much future anguish – and about prevention, which is now, thankfully, possible.

Among the most difficult people to help are women who suffer from what they vaguely call 'nerves'. Doctors often suggest that psychiatric treatment could help, and that's when the nervous women write. The very mention of the dreaded word 'psychiatrist' conjures up visions of raving madness, of padded cells and years, perhaps the rest of life, inside a mental hospital.

Q. I am desperately worried. For a long time I have been suffering from nervous troubles brought about, my doctor thinks, by a very unhappy childhood and broken home. Now he has suggested I should see a psychiatrist. Does this mean he thinks that my mind is affected? Though he is kind, he is a busy doctor and sometimes he seems impatient. I don't want to take up his time and wonder if you would mind telling me what you think. In plain words, do you suppose my doctor believes I'm going mad?

A. Most people who are advised to seek psychiatric help feel as frightened as you do – but many keep their fears to themselves. Which is, in fact, crazy. I do not for a moment think you are going mad. Neither, I'm sure, does your doctor. He is simply doing what every wise GP does: referring you to a consultant who specialises in a particular medical field.

There is a lot of mystery surrounding mental illness. People are sometimes more afraid of it than they are of physical illness, though there's no reason why they should be.

I can reassure you, I hope, by telling you you're very lucky to have a doctor who sees that you can be helped by going to the right man. Try to see it this way: if you had a physical illness that didn't respond quickly to treatment by your doctor, you would be grateful to him for referring you to a specialist. Likewise with a mental illness or disorder: that, too, often needs specialist treatment.

People who neglect to seek help are much more likely to lose their reason than those who are too afraid to see a psychiatrist. You are going to see this man to save your health. Put yourself trustingly in his capable and experienced hands.

Agoraphobia is one of the nervous ailments from which thousands of women suffer and because they are apparently in good physical health, they get little, if any sympathy from their families. Impatient husbands and children cannot understand why a perfectly fit woman trembles with fear at the prospect of leaving the house. Women describe breaking out into cold sweats, fainting as they approach the front door, clinging to shop doorways and railings if they manage to force themselves to stagger to the corner shop.

'I have tried so hard,' wrote one wife, 'to overcome these senseless feelings. The doctor tells me to try to pull myself together. My husband says I behave like a neurotic fool, that I am lucky not to have to go out to work like most women and accuses me of being idle. "Occupy your mind," he says, "and you won't have so much time to invent illnesses and nerves." He goes out more and more, leaving me alone and I can see why he gets so impatient, but if he left me altogether, I would be quite helpless. My only daughter is married. . . .'

There is little that can be done for women like this. Various organisations and societies exist which can offer not much more than an exchange of letters from suffering sisters, or cheery newsletters to boost morale.

Hardly any money is spent on research into this and other phobias. The sufferers have no lively pressure groups to promote research, or collect money for it. As another agoraphobic wrote, 'If we were spastics, if we could be seen to be sick, perhaps public sympathy – let alone sympathy within the family – might be aroused.'

As for me, with memories of an agoraphobic mother, I can certainly offer sympathy, but wish I could offer more practical

6•

advice. Whenever there's an opportunity to arouse family sympathy for such women, I take it. The following letter provided just such a chance. . . .

Q. I have the misfortune to be married to a hypochondriac. She collects illnesses like other women collect cookery recipes. Whatever's wrong with anyone else, she gets the symptoms right away. If a neighbour has a sick headache – she gets it, too. If I have a cold, she complains about her sore throat. The house is rattling with pills and medicine bottles and her imaginary sicknesses are making ME ill. When she can't think of anything else to complain about there's always her nerves or her agoraphobia.

A. Have you ever wondered why your wife invents these illnesses of which you complain? Presumably, she's perfectly healthy physically, for I imagine you'd have called in the doctor if you'd felt that she was truly suffering from any of the illnesses she appears to invent. Or would you? You are very unsympathetic and hard – which may be one reason behind the problem. Perhaps your wife is hungry for love and attention. These imagined illnesses could well be her way of saying, 'Love me – and show it. Show me how much you want me and need me.'

The cure for her imaginary diseases could be in your hands. Try the medicine I prescribe. Show her the kindness you would expect if you were ill – for she *is* ill. And I think you will see a rapid improvement.

As Young as You Think

It is often said that people are as old as they feel. In my opinion, it is also often wrongly said: people, I believe, are as old as they *think*. But in the youth-orientated culture in which we live, it is hardly surprising that people in their forties often feel old.

Our life style pays homage to youth. Clothing, cosmetic and record manufacturers are geared to a young, free-spending market. Cosmetic firms sell their products on a stay-young-and-beautiful theme. The entertainment industry focuses on youthful crazes and promotes crazes directed specifically towards the young.

It seems to many that the old are not worth cultivating. And old can mean any age over forty-five. Women, particularly, are the victims of youth worship in all sorts of ways. When the bloom fades, they are conditioned by propaganda to believe that attractiveness fades too. They cling desperately to their youthful image in the fear of losing out in competition for men, or in the fear of losing their men to younger, more desirable women. They buy expensive cosmetic aids, urged by advertisers to look young and stay young. Often it's their very anxieties about growing old which produce the wrinkles and the taut lines of premature ageing. They lie about their ages to deceive themselves as well as others.

Many men, too, become obsessed by fear of age, though in my experience their reasons are different. They are more afraid of losing jobs and prestige than of losing their looks. They are very afraid indeed of losing their sexual virility, of becoming impotent and useless.

Both men and women are fearful of becoming burdens on their families or on society, of being unwanted and rejected. But as I see it, old age is often an attitude and a frame of mind. There are women who are 'mumsy' at twenty and old at thirty-five, men in their thirties who are less youthful than lively seventy-year-olds.

The young 'olds' never do anything impulsive, never take risks, are contemptuous of fun-loving citizens, are neither inquisitive, imaginative nor inventive. They are conformists, often bigoted and intolerant. Their attitudes grow even harder as they become old in years and they are usually, in the end, casualties of their inability to think young.

But many older people maintain a remarkable zest for life for as long as it lasts, cheerfully enduring the diminution of physical functioning, exercising their minds, even though their bodies inevitably slow up.

Once, when I was dieting to get rid of excess poundage, a friend sent me a telegram which said THINK THIN. It helped me much more than the dog-eared calorie chart I'd been poring over for weeks. That short, sharp message inspired me to pass on a similar one to those who write about the fears and depression the advancing years produce. THINK YOUNG is the message. It isn't going to make the ravages of age disappear the way the 'think thin' injunction helped to cut my hips back to size, but many people have told me that it has changed their attitude to ageing, has made them think more positively and usefully.

Two major areas of anxiety are underlined in my letters from older citizens: the problems surrounding retirement – for both women and men; and diminishing sexuality, which brings complications deeper than the actual lessening of the sex drive.

Retirement problems increase as men retire younger and younger. When it was confidently assumed that a man would continue to work until he was sixty-five, he and his wife were usually able to condition themselves to a change of life style. The ideal prospect for many was a small bungalow near the sea with a spare room for visiting children and grandchildren and a settling down to tranquil twilight years at the end of a life of hard work. But in the past few years, many men have been forced into retirement in their mid-fifties. Almost all of them suffer from a sense of rejection and uselessness, feeling that while still comparatively young and vigorous, they are on the scrap heap.

Apart from money, they miss job satisfaction and the companionship of other workers. They miss the status and authority in the home which their jobs earned them. They are lost. Idleness eats away at their morale, particularly if they are married, as so many are, to younger wives still working. A healthy man who retires young could be facing up to twenty or more years of an entirely different style of life for which he is unlikely to be equipped.

Waking up one morning to the realisation that he is not needed, that he is going to be under his wife's feet – or bidding her goodbye as he sees her off to work, is deeply demoralising. There is still too little thought and preparation for retirement provided for such men, either by society or by themselves. Retirement, therefore, can mark the beginning of the end for a still virile, active man. Without hobbies and with no preparation for the future, it looks bleak and arid.

When such men – or their wives – write to me for advice as to how to fill their days or cope with the years ahead, there is little I can suggest. Wives, I think, could be more helpful than many are. Women resent the upheaval of their organised routine. They write complaining of the man now under their feet. They object to cooking midday meals where once they nibbled a sandwich in the kitchen. They find domestic jobs for their husbands to do: sending them to the shops for errands, putting the vacuum cleaner in their hands, snapping back at the grumbling man when he objects to being given domestic tasks to keep him occupied. Wives, often coping with their own menopausal problems, have little patience to deal with a man whose presence all day in the home is a reminder to them of their own approaching old age. . . .

Q. I am very worried about my husband's coming retirement. His job has been his one interest in life and now, at fifty-five, the firm has asked him to retire early. He says he's been put on the scrap heap and he's harder to live with daily. What am I going to do when he's under my feet all day? Do you think he might settle down or should I persuade him to try to get another job?

A. It's obvious that you both have to adapt to a new life style. Not just your husband, but you, too. You seem to have little, if any, sympathy for a man who feels he's been rejected. Your main concern is that he's going to get under your feet. I am not surprised, if this has been your attitude, that his job has been his main interest in life.

I do not think you'll have much trouble persuading him to look for another job, for I doubt if he'll want to spend all day at home any more than you want him to. But I advise you to be very careful how you go about your persuading. If you add to his feeling of humiliation and failure by saying you want him out from under your feet, he's still young enough, remember, to get out from under them permanently. But if you can try to reassure him, telling him he's a real loss to industry with his skills or talents or knowledge or whatever, he might begin to feel less miserable.

He may not, of course, find it easy to get another job. But there is a crying need for voluntary workers in all sorts of fields where he would soon feel wanted and valuable. He ought to feel wanted and valuable at home, too, and you'd be a fool not to realise what damage you can do to him and to your marriage by treating him as a nuisance.

Both men and women face daunting problems in middle age which can, and often do, threaten or even break their marriages. The divorce rate shoots up among those who have been married twenty years or more. Menopausal women become increasingly irritable; children who have kept them busy leave home. Husbands are downright tiresome.

It's during this period that many a man looks around for the consolation of a younger, less sharp-tongued woman. Or one who will reassure him that age has not withered him. Many men are convinced that, like women, they have a menopause, an actual physical as well as an emotional change of life between forty-five and fifty-five. They use it as an excuse for lack of drive. But there is no medical evidence to support the 'male menopause' theory.

There is a steady decline in the ability to get and maintain an erection, but there are no hormone changes comparable with that of women whose ovulation and production of oestrogen ceases during the few years of menopause. But both men and women at this time of change, physical or psychological – or both – are at their most vulnerable, dreading the onset of age and the rejection it so often brings.

For women, the change is often an eagerly grasped opportunity to reject sex. A woman who has always merely endured it as part of the duties of matrimony will use her menopausal symptoms as an excuse to say no. She has one of her regular headaches or a punishing backache. She feels, she says, too tired and depressed for love-making and complains of her husband's selfish lack of consideration in making demands at her time of life. She may genuinely have these symptoms but they are good excuses for refusing intercourse. In addition, penetration is sometimes painful during menopause but instead of going to her doctor for help, she puts up with the symptoms which she regards as only to be expected at her time of life.

In fact, in recent years great strides have been made in this field of medicine and I advise women who write to ask their doctors about hormone replacement therapy which can work what would once have been thought of as miracles. Replacement therapy can not only reduce the menopausal symptoms or even banish them, but can effectively delay the ageing processes of the body and skin, providing physical relief as well as a psychological boost to the morale.

The woman who grasps the symptoms as an excuse to avoid intercourse will be resistant to seeking help which might take away her excuse. But countless women in middle age who long to continue a normal sexual relationship are eager to get help. A radio programme in which I participated in a discussion about hormone replacement therapy with a gynaecologist, produced thousands of pleas from women listeners for information about how they could get it. We said they should ask their doctors for advice – and refuse to be put off by a doctor who says, 'The change is a perfectly natural function, Mrs So and So. Go away and learn to live with it.' Not all doctors are enthusiastic about hormone therapy; some believe there are possible risks attached to it. But I have had a gratifying response from women who have written to say, 'The pills my doctor prescribed (or the oestrogen implant) have saved my marriage . . .'

One of the commonest questions women ask about the menopause is, 'When is it safe to have intercourse without taking contraceptive precautions?' In most cases, the answer is two years after the last period, provided there's been no show of blood during the two years. The fact that so many women want to know this indicates that sexual activity doesn't decline for a comfortingly high proportion of older people.

It's to be hoped that, as the image of the sexless elderly and of what has been believed in the past to be their inevitable sexual decay fades, more and more older citizens will continue to enjoy sex. Folklore and myths have created the image; scientists are dispelling it, proving that sex can do nothing but good for the healthy, whatever their age.

One of the problems older people face is the condemnatory attitudes of their grown-up children who subscribe to the view that sex between their elders is unseemly, thus perpetuating the myth which brings so much unhappiness for those whose lives could be enriched by fulfilling companionship. The idea that older people might be anything more than platonically in love is often seen as an indecency.

Q. At the age of fifty-six, my mother has suddenly changed from a sensible, dignified widow into a vulgar laughing stock. She is having an affair with a younger man (in his forties) who often stays the night at her home.

It isn't that my brother and I (both married) mind her having a friend, but we have tried to explain that he can only be after the money our father left her, which wasn't really very much. She says we don't understand. Sadly we understand only too well what is happening. How can we warn her before it's too late?

A. You understand, say you and your self-righteous brother, what this affair is all about. That's what you think. What I think is that you haven't the first glimmering of understanding. You have a lot of impertinence, though, in trying to break up a friendship which is giving your mother new excitement and interest in her life. At fifty-six, she is still young enough to enjoy a man's company and love-making. And at fifty-six, she is old enough to know what she is doing. She is not a dewy-eyed girl in love for the first time. As you say, she is a sensible woman.

You mention that you and your brother – both married and presumably therefore not able to give your mother much of your time and attention – don't mind her having a friend. It is decent of you not to mind. In fact, it's none of your business. Even if this man *is* after her bit of money, I dare say she's aware of it and won't be silly enough to part with her cash. Even if she did, though, she might just figure she is getting her money's worth.

Maybe I've been somewhat harsh with you, but I do get angry when grown-up children treat their parents like doddering fools who have no sense and no judgement. I'm sure you are concerned about your mother's future but don't get carried away by this image of dignified, sensible widowhood. If her lover provides her with company and consolation, be thankful that your mother has found some cheerful purpose in living.

*

Q. I have been a widow since I was sixty and now I am sixty-five. I loved my husband and we had a good life together. I still miss him and feel very lonely at times. Not long ago I met a widower in his seventies at a club and he has asked me to marry him. We get on well and it would be lovely to care for someone again. But my friends and family say it's not nice and that I am behaving like a silly old fool. Do you agree with them? I may be a fool, but for the first time in five years I am truly happy.

A. Your friends and family are the fools, while you are a very wise and lovely lady. Your gentleman friend is lucky to have found you. After years of happy marriage, of course you are lonely and longing to care for a man again. And why shouldn't you?

I know a lady in her late sixties who acquired a lover. You aren't about to disgrace your family by doing anything as outrageous as that. You marry your gentleman, and take care of him and let him take care of you – and ignore the selfish and unimaginative remarks of those around you. One day they, too, may discover what loneliness is – and wish they had a loving companion with whom they could spend their twilight years.

The question of remarriage in later life crops up frequently. Both men and women, widowed or divorced perhaps for years, and after years of sexual abstinence, worry about their prospects for a new marriage. Research has shown that elderly married partners are likely to be much better off in health than those who remain single. Married couples tend to eat better, take more care of each other and of themselves and are mentally stimulated by each other. They go out more, see more people and have a wider social life, generally, than elderly loners.

When a man in his late sixties, hovering on the brink of a proposal to a widow around the same age, writes to me asking whether he should or shouldn't, I am happy to tell him that the marriage could well prolong both their lives and that their twilight years will be all the more rewarding for being shared. Problems can arise, however, when one or both partners have established a life style to which the other is unable or unwilling to adapt and where both refuse to compromise, which is something older people are often reluctant to try to do.

Q. I have been a widower for several years and, at the age of sixty-two, have become friendly with a widow two years my junior. She is very keen to remarry. But lately I have been irritated by her attitude. She seems determined to make me a carbon copy of her late husband, even to trying to persuade me to take up golf and smoke his brand of cigarettes, but I have my own ways and I won't change to suit anyone. I don't intend being a replacement for the man she lost five years ago. Do you think I should retreat before getting any more deeply involved?

A. I would be very careful, if I were you, about making a final commitment for the time being. I am suspicious about your friend's motives for wanting to marry you. Like you, I have a powerful feeling she is simply seeking another version of her late husband rather than a new, live flesh and blood man. Maybe she doesn't realise it herself. Perhaps her efforts to get you to be like him are a subconscious longing for the safe and happy life she once led with him. Perhaps she is secretly afraid to meet the challenge of life with a stranger.

But don't just sit there quietly seething. Be bold and talk it all out with her. Explain that in order to be a good man for her, you must be your own man. There is a chance then, I think, that she will realise that in trying to change you, she is in danger of losing you.

There is one point upon which I must take issue with you: you won't change, you say, to suit anyone. That's as foolish an attitude as hers. Everyone who contemplates marriage must be prepared to change and adapt. If you refuse to try, I give very little hope for your happiness with this woman – or any other.

Often, as the ageing process diminishes sexuality, the still active partner suspects that the one whose ardour has cooled has found someone else. . . .

Q. At the age of fifty-seven, I am no longer as sexually virile as I used to be. Sometimes all goes well, but often, however hard I try to make love to my wife, I cannot manage it. She certainly does her best to stimulate me but has now started questioning my fidelity to her. She seems to suspect that the reason I am not able to satisfy her is because I am making love to someone else. This is totally untrue and her suspicions anger me because, except for one brief foolish episode, twenty years ago (which she discovered), I've never looked at another woman. We quarrel a good deal these days and I'll confess I lose my temper with her for her lack of understanding of a condition that's likely to occur to many men of my age. I would value your advice about this unhappy state of affairs.

A. Your wife is reacting to your reduced virility in a perfectly predictable way. Many women, in similar circumstances, begin to wonder if another woman is the reason for her husband's inability to respond. I dare say your earlier infidelity still rankles, even after all these years. Wives never forget, though they may forgive.

The present trouble with your relationship, I think, is not so much your sexual failure as your irritable attitude towards your wife. If you were loving rather than cross, you'd be likely to get sympathy instead of suspicion. She must surely realise that failure is likely to occur to men of your age. If she doesn't, explain to her that the sexual threshold of most men declines much earlier than that of women, while many women continue to be enthusiastic and sometimes even more responsive as they grow older.

But actions being even more important than words in such a situation, I advise you to be as demonstrative as you know how. I also advise you to make love to her even when you are not, yourself, able physically to satisfy her in the usually accepted way. Any imaginative man can arouse and satisfy his wife – even if he is totally impotent. If you cannot use your penis to satisfy her, there are other ways. Manual clitoral stimulation will bring her to a climax. Concentrate on her needs, but, above all, reassure her. Tell her how much you love her and need her help and sympathy. And don't lose your temper, for it's vitally important for both of you to understand each other at this particularly difficult time of your lives.

A good many older men, alarmed by their inability to achieve and sustain an erection, write about their deep anxiety and their fears of total impotence. Often the anxieties are the very cause of the trouble and the more fraught the man becomes, the less chance he will have of performing effectively. I remind anxious men that impotence can be linked to general debility. The man who is run down, gets over-tired, fails to take regular exercise, drinks excessively or is taking pills or drugs or sedatives will inevitably, as he gets older, experience a diminishing of his sexual drive.

An understanding wife can help to combat the problem just as a querulous, scornful or demanding wife can exacerbate it. A change of position in intercourse is sometimes helpful, with the woman lying on top of the man which allows him to insert and keep in position even a partially erect penis. If the women provides most of the initial rhythmic movements, it is sometimes possible for the man to maintain his erection and subsequently, to ejaculate.

A huge bogey for women in middle age is what they often describe as 'trouble down below', which necessitates the removal of the uterus or the ovaries or the lot. Only too ready to listen to horror stories which friends and neighbours are eager to impart, the terrified woman listens with growing apprehension to the inaccurate old wives' tales. Ignorant, usually, of what the operation means, of what the surgeon will do to her while she is under the anaesthetic, she is convinced that if she's lucky enough to live through it, life won't be much worth living after it anyway.

A gynaecologist – one who is very sensitive indeed to the psychological, as well as the physical effects of the operation, told me that one of the most difficult problems which he has to combat is the enshrined attitudes of his patients to the operation. They regale him with the horror stories and he has a hard time convincing them that there are dozens of different reasons why women need this operation, that symptoms vary in different women and that the job the surgeon does is specific to each patient. He regards it as part of his treatment to reassure women that a hysterectomy does not mean instant ageing and the end of matrimonial happiness. With the touch of earthy vulgarity

I've noted in several gynaecologists, he tells them, 'I shall be taking away the cradle – but leaving behind the play-pen. And you'll be able to enjoy all the old games with even more enthusiasm in the future.'

For the majority of women, a hysterectomy is a turning-point in their age span. They believe they will be less feminine, less desirable (or not desirable at all), that they will age rapidly, get stout and go to seed. The woman who subconsciously believes that sex is solely for the procreation of children feels deeply maimed when she realises that she has lost her main feminine motivation and many such women tell me of their feeling of utter uselessness, despair and depression.

Most of the letters I write to women who are about to undergo or have recently undergone a hysterectomy are factual and aimed at scotching the myths and at reassuring them. Reinforced by medical opinion, I can tell them that their skin won't suddenly sag, nor will their hair go grey overnight because of the operation, that normal ageing processes will do that to it anyway – and what's wrong with subtle tinting? I suggest that once over convalescence, a second honeymoon would be a great idea and assure them that it's likely to be a lot better than their first, for they'll have a wealth of experience behind them and none of the old fears of an unwanted pregnancy to worry about. They'll feel better in health than they have done for years and with the right cheerful, optimistic frame of mind, life can be much more rewarding and exciting as a result of the surgeon's skill.

A good many women, believing that they'll turn overnight into ageing, wrinkled, scarecrows, fear that their husbands will 'go off' them. They have nightmare visions of him fleeing to the arms of a younger woman – especially since wives are sure their hysterectomy will mean that they'll lose all interest in sex, as well as their sexual appeal.

When women write to me before the operation, I can help to put their fears to rest. But all too often, their attitude towards it puts them at the very risk they most fear . . . and they write when the damage has already been done.

Q. When I learned I needed to have a hysterectomy, I was out of my mind with worry. I have been married twenty-three years and until about three years ago (when I was forty-six), we were very happy and our sex life was good. Then I began to have severe bleeding and very painful periods and naturally, during this time, I didn't feel like love-making. I have never been one to make a fuss and I made light of my troubles as far as I could and my husband didn't guess the real reason why I preferred to sleep alone. I realise how foolish I was, for I didn't even tell him at the time that I was regularly consulting the doctor. He apparently believed that I'd grown disinterested and our relationship became very strained.

I always felt at low ebb and was irritable and the inevitable happened. He found someone else to sleep with. I blame myself for not telling him the truth, for he is a kind man and I think now that he would have been patient. We are still living together, although I think he still sees the other woman occasionally. He doesn't realise that I know about the affair, which I discovered quite by chance. I am sure, too, that he cares for me, for he is very concerned and sympathetic about the operation I am waiting to have, and seems genuinely worried about me. I know he won't leave me now, not at any rate until I am well again, as the surgeon assures me I will be, but I dread the future and sometimes hope I'll never wake up from the anaesthetic.

A. You are right when you say how foolish you have been but nothing is to be gained by brooding about past errors. From what you say of your husband, the future looks better to me than you imagine it could.

I believe that if you can face the operation optimistically, you can face the future optimistically, too. You have your doctor's assurance that you will get well. You will, in fact, be better than you have been for the past few years. You must explain to your husband the reasons why you became withdrawn. He sounds the sort of man who could understand. His present attitude underlines his hopes for your recovery and I'm sure he'd be horrified if he knew the depths of your misery.

It seems to me that your marriage has a very good chance of survival and I advise you to try to get away, with your husband, as soon as your doctor agrees. You'd better go on pretending you know nothing about the infidelity. It sounds like a pretty casual affair anyway, simply an outlet, I imagine, for your husband's frustrated sexual needs. He'd have left you long before now if he'd had a deep commitment to the other woman.

My prophecy is that he'll be anxiously waiting for you to open your eyes and become conscious of him. And you must stay that way and let him see that you need him and want him. If I were a betting lady, I'd stake heavily on your prospects for a happy future together.

Few young married couples, as they begin to negotiate the bumpy matrimonial road at the start of their marriage, stop to contemplate what life may be like as they arrive towards the end of it. If they ever did look that far ahead, they might, perhaps, see themselves in a rosy dream of a rose-covered cottage – a gracious Darby and Joan pair, hand in hand, still in love, still beautiful people – and rich with it.

In reality, the knocks people take along that bumpy road, the struggles they meet, the troubles they face, the battles of survival they fight, leave deep telling scars. Darby and Joan are as likely as not to be a hard-up, sour and cantankerous old couple, warring with their families and often with each other, subconsciously resentful that the years have robbed them of their beauty and vitality, resentful of missed opportunities and frustrated ambition, and deeply afraid of death, the unmentionable taboo word. But when all passion is finally spent, if they can look at each other and think, 'Well, at least we've still got each other,' they *are* rich.

The biggest blessing of old age is a partner to share it with – which is what I tell the grumblers who write about the shortcomings of their ageing partners. And sometimes even get a grudging 'Yes, you're right, I suppose,' reply.

A letter I once had from a newly widowed lady will always stay sharply in my mind. I had published a wife's request for a cure for her husband's high-decibel snoring. 'It's driving me mad,' she'd written. 'Night after night I'm awake listening to this terrible sound and sometimes I feel I could smother him with the pillow. . . .' The widow, on reading of this commonplace, nightly disturbance in a million matrimonial bedrooms, wrote, 'I, too, used to lie awake distraught by my late husband's dreadful snoring. Now I lie awake and stare at the place in our bed that he occupied and I would give anything to have him back, snoring his head off beside me.'

Women in a Man's World

Changes in society are bound to bring changes in the kind of problems which beset people. While the basic human problems do not alter over comparatively short periods, one change over the past few years has made dramatic impact: it is the change in the status of women. More than anything else, it has created new attitudes and new dilemmas in relationships. It has altered the balance of family life and produced a whole new range of tensions in male-female pairing.

In one year – 1975 – women saw the formalised end to a struggle for equality that formally began in 1888, when the Trades Union Council passed the first resolution demanding equal pay for women workers. In 1975, women became officially and legally 'equal', when the hard fought for Anti-Discrimination laws and the Equal Pay Act went into the statute books.

The near hundred years' struggle was a long hard one, fought on behalf of the many by the few. Where the brave suffragettes at the beginning of the present century left off, the militant women's liberationists took over in the sixties. Ridiculed and condemned by men and women alike, the noisy minority struggled to make life fairer and sweeter and more just for the silent and often hostile majority. Their greatest enemies in their fight to improve the status of women were women themselves. Apathetic and indifferent or angry, the mass of women in western society have not, on the whole, shown gratitude to the liberationists – except in one area: they are deeply grateful for equal pay packets. But when it comes to facing the pressures that earning those pay packets bring, their problems are immense.

Nearly half of all married women are now working outside

the home but few of them see themselves as women striking a blow for female progress and freedom. Mainly, they work to augment the family's finances, to provide clothes and pocket money for their children, to maintain a reasonable standard of living at a time when it's no longer possible for huge numbers of families to manage adequately on one pay packet.

For the majority of wives, the idea propounded by the liberation movement of job fulfilment and career prospects is a grim joke. Career women, professional women, who have interesting jobs, who can afford help in the home, and have supportive husbands proud of their wives' achievements are a tiny minority of the female work force. For most, the 'fulfilling' job means a life of slavery: doing the housework before and after work, shopping in the lunch break, lugging home heavy bags, cooking early in the morning before rushing off to catch buses or trains, tearing home to feed the family. A 'fulfilling' job means anxiety, guilt and, as one woman described it, 'soul and body-destroying fatigue'. She wrote, 'I am too tired to do my job properly, too tired for my children, too tired for love-making, too tired, even, to talk. Yet I must continue to work, for with all the will in the world and even though I'm a good manager, we cannot cope on my husband's salary. I know my marriage is suffering because of it, but what can I do?'

One of the more damaging problems brought about by increased pressures on women to contribute to the family's finances is the fact that many women work unsocial hours, doing two full-time jobs. They choose to go out to work at night in factories or as waitresses or cleaners so that they can be mothers during the day.

Typical of the stresses such a way of life can bring is the story one woman told me. Her husband went to his job in the morning and she got her children off to school. During the day she shopped, cleaned, cooked, washed and ironed. She saw her children briefly at lunch time and again briefly after school. She left an evening meal in the oven ready for her husband to cook when he returned from work and, on his return, left the house to do her job as an office cleaner. When she got home, her husband was usually in bed and asleep. They had almost no contact. Her husband worked Saturdays. Sunday was a day of exhaustion.

Women like this laugh bitterly when they hear high-sounding talk about job-fulfilment and career prospects. If they have any ambition, it's to stay at home and be housewives and do one fulfilling job well – that of being a wife and mother.

But the housewives who *do* stay at home are also influenced by the change in women's status. They read articles or listen to broadcasts by feminists who tell them that the housewife role is degrading slavery. They are urged to broaden their horizons, to become valuable citizens rather than domestic cabbages. They become confused and doubtful. Should they get a job so as to be more interesting wives and mothers? If they are young women, they miss the companionship of workmates and they miss the independence their salaries gave them. What they find degrading is having to ask a man for every pound and to beg, as they often tell me, for the price of a once-a-month hairdo.

There's another disturbing aspect beginning to creep into the women and work situation: more and more men, wives say, are actually demanding and insisting that their wives go out to work. 'Mrs So and So manages to do a job and run the house,' men say. 'Why can't you help out?' Women have told me their husbands call them lazy if they refuse to do a job outside the home. . . .

Q. Last week I had to ask my husband for an increase in my housekeeping allowance, which I know he can well afford. He never deprives himself of anything. His answer was that I should go out and get a job like other women. I have brought up four boys, three of whom are still at home. I do all the housework and get no help. I am nearly fifty-five. When I said a job was out of the question, my husband called me lazy.

A. In many cases the family does need the extra cash a working wife brings home. But your husband seems to be particularly unreasonable. I can imagine your indignation when he called you lazy. You do not say whether or not you answered back by pointing out his selfishness.

Your husband must be made to realise that if you go out to work he will get a less efficient service at home. And you would be entitled to expect him to cut back on his personal spending and do his share of the chores. Frankly, he doesn't sound the sort who would co-operate, which leaves you little choice. Either you must try to get a job, maintain your standard of living and let the housework and cooking slide, or dig in your heels and endeavour to get him to see things realistically. The only one who can really help you is your husband. It is time that he, and others like him, recognised the problems wives face today – and did his fair share to relieve the pressures and burdens.

But the attitude of a vast majority of husbands, despite legal 'equality' and the generally changed thinking towards women working, remains one of resentment. There is still a hard core of men, mostly among the middle-aged and older husbands, who maintain that women's rightful place is in the home and mostly the kitchen and who blame (with truth) the women's rights movement for making wives restless and discontented with their homemaking role.

Q. For ten years, my marriage has been very happy. My wife is a marvellous, sexy girl and a first-class cook and house-keeper and hostess and I am the envy of my friends because of the way she runs our home. Our only regret is that we are unable to have children but we have come to terms with that. Lately, my wife has been quiet and moody and the other night, to my astonishment, she said she intended to get a job, that she was sick of being a domestic drudge, that she was a slave to my stomach and she had no intention of devoting her whole life to pleasing me. I blame Women's Lib ideas for making women like my wife so discontented. If she carries out her threat, it will ruin our marriage.

A. Don't blame the liberationists entirely. Be a man and shoulder at least some of the blame yourself. Blame your own lack of imagination, your selfishness and your demanding stomach for your wife's disenchantment with your idea of domestic bliss – which clearly isn't hers.

It is men like you who stimulate their wives' interest in Women's Lib. The movement gathered force as more and more women all over the world began to feel that being housebound was stultifying. Many women *are* happy to be at home and good luck to them and I am the first one to say that if they find domesticity bliss, it's splendid for them and for their families. But if a woman feels that being tied to a home and a cooker is slavery, she ought to be encouraged by her husband to extend her narrow horizons.

Keeping your wife chained to the kitchen is not going to save your marriage. Helping her to discover her other talents might. If you insist on frustrating her urge to go out to work, her moods will become blacker and her cooking will deteriorate along with your relationship.

You should support her ambition for both your sakes. At least give her a chance to find out if she'd be happier working. Though after a few months of competing in the tough hard world outside the shelter of her home, she may be very glad to return to it. Just stop taking it for granted that every woman is beside herself with joy and gratitude to be a man's servile creature. You could have a lovely marriage if only you'd treat her as a citizen with human rights and not as a household pet.

It isn't only husbands who are often resistant to women going out to work. Many employers are resistant, too, unless their businesses depend on a female labour force. Laws may make it illegal to discriminate against women employees, but laws are slow to change attitudes which have been ingrained for generations.

Most men secretly and some overtly believe women to be inferior second-class citizens, but because it is no longer acceptable to be able, publicly, to state their opinion, they find all sorts of reasons why women are less satisfactory employees. They are not reliable, go the myths; they are not really interested in the job, only in the money; they regard jobs as fillers between school and marriage; there is more absenteeism among women; it isn't worth spending cash and time training them to be more than shorthand typists or shop assistants for they are not likely to stick to a good job which requires responsibility.

All this is true of some women but it is not true of the majority, especially not of younger women who believe themselves to be as capable, reliable, intelligent and conscientious as their equivalent men.

One of the most specious arguments is about women in medicine. I have debated fiercely with deans and professors about the quota which has militated against female medical students in teaching hospitals and university faculties. The old excuse is revived every time: 'Why spend money training a girl to be a doctor when the chances are she'll get married and have children within a year or so of qualifying? Male students don't drop out when they marry.' In fact many women doctors return to practice after they have borne their children and continue to work for years, while a huge number of male doctors emigrate on qualifying.

If there is prejudice on the part of employers, husbands and the professors which ambitious women have to combat, there is also sometimes prejudice among parents. Some are ambitious for their daughters, and proud of their successes, but some, with deeply ingrained notions about women's rightful domestic role, express grave doubts when their daughters announce an intention to pursue a career rather than a husband. A lot of fathers think that training girls for careers is a waste of money, but mothers worry more about the 'unnatural' attitudes of career-seeking daughters. . . .

Q. My daughter, aged twenty-six, is a very good business woman. She has a well-paid job and is saving towards starting her own company. She is an attractive girl, with plenty of casual boy friends but because of working long hours, she never has a steady relationship.

I want her to marry and have a family and lead a normal life but she scoffs at my anxiety for her future. She says marriage is not the only objective for a woman. How can I prove to her that she's so wrong?

A. I do not think you have the right to try to prove your point, despite your anxiety for your daughter's future. Neither am I as certain as you are that marriage is the only worthwhile objective for a woman. It is for some, of course, but there are many women who do not feel that acquiring a husband and children is the only goal worth reaching.

If you did manage to get her to look at it from your point of view, you could propel her into a marriage which could turn out to be a disaster. Would you rather she was married and miserable or single and happy?

She may yet fall in love; love changes a girl's outlook more effectively than a mother's anxious pleas. Perhaps, in the end, she will do what so many ambitious women do: manage to combine a career with family life. That is the ideal, if she is lucky enough to find a man who supports her theories.

But you ought to stop putting pressures on her, for there is no longer any stigma attached to spinsterhood. She is entitled to make her own choice, and from what you say of her, intelligent enough to know what she's doing.

The changing status of women has made dramatic differences to their relationships with men, both social and sexual. Girls no longer feel they must wait to be asked by a man for dates. When I first began to write an advice column, it was commonplace to be asked by a girl how she could get a particular boy to invite her out. Such letters today are very rare, even among insecure teenagers. Girls have become bold, will telephone boys for dates, think nothing of turning down invitations from boys or refusing to dance with men they don't care for. More and more women show their disinterest in or contempt for men who regard them as mere sex objects to be exploited. There is, in fact, an increasing tendency on the part of women to make demands on men, demands which men are not always able to meet. Women's new-found independence and the assurance they have steadily gained is producing a curious backlash.

The more aggressive, the more independent, the more liberated women become, the more they put men at risk, psychologically and sexually. Studies made in the United States have shown that the male ego has been so bruised and damaged and emasculated by liberated women that many men have actually become impotent and the cause of their impotency has been traced to the denigration of their masculinity by demanding women. Not only, it was found, were men unable to participate in intercourse – they did not even want to try. It appeared that many men had abdicated their male role and felt themselves to be in an inferior position to women.

Some psychiatrists in this country with whom I have discussed this possible backlash to the women's movement have told me that they, too, see signs of it happening and they maintain that as the sexual liberation of women gains ground here, it is similarly affecting British husbands and lovers. No longer submissive, no longer demurely waiting for the man to make the first move, women have become sexual instigators, taking the initiative where once they waited to be taken.

Q. Women seem to me to be changed creatures. In the past, if a man made his sexual intentions plain, a girl would keep him waiting for weeks before giving in. Or she would tell him he was interested only in her for sex. Now, most girls seem to look on sex as their right. If they haven't been satisfied within the first couple of meetings, if a man has failed to impress a girl with his sexual expertise, he is a loser.

I went out with a girl a few times recently without trying to make love to her, although I admit it was in my mind. She actually asked me if I found her unattractive and undesirable. Believe it or not, I was treating her to some old-fashioned respect.

A. You seem to be meeting the wrong types for a man like yourself who clearly prefers the delights of the chase. It is true that the girls who once gave in to an importunate man with some show of coy reluctance are getting scarcer and scarcer. More and more females are taking the view that sexual gratification is no longer a one-sided affair. The new-found freedom of women and their increasing resentment about male domination is encouraging them to take the initiative in all sorts of areas, including sex. And when you think of it, why indeed should it be the male prerogative to make the running?

If a man attracts a girl, can you think of a good reason, really, why she should fail to make it clear to him? There are no laws (or only man-made ones) which require a woman to wait meekly to be asked.

I realise that masculine vanity prefers feminine mock modesty, it's all part of the double standard which men have maintained for so long. Time is running out, though. It may not be long before men will be heard plaintively saying to girls, 'You're only interested in me for sex.' And men will wonder where they heard those familiar words before.

There have always been dominating women and hen-pecked men. They are standard old vaudeville jokes, like mothers-in-law. But female domination has taken on a new dimension with the increasing sexual demands women are now making. In the past, when women were mainly dominated by men, it was commonplace for women to accept that theirs was the pleasure-giving role, while their lovers enjoyed fulfilment.

In the majority of cases, the male climax signalled the end and also the success of love-making. But the sexual enlightenment of women and the contraceptive pill which gives them sexual freedom, has resulted in a whole new range of expectations. Women now expect and demand fulfilment for themselves. Unless they achieve orgasm during intercourse, they feel cheated and deprived. If their physical requirements are not met, they do not hesitate to blame their husbands and lovers for lack of expertise.

Many men have written to tell me that their wives and girl friends have complained if fulfilment isn't forthcoming. Many men are unable to satisfy demanding women, and have asked for advice about useful techniques. But all the talk about increasing feminine demands disturbs some women, too. . . .

Q. We have heard so much about a woman's right to fulfilled sex and how cheated and bitter she becomes if she is frustrated. But I seldom reach a climax, even after five years of happy marriage to a wonderfully considerate husband. I must say that it never bothers me and I always enjoy our love-making and take pleasure in helping him to achieve satisfaction. Is orgasm really so strong a need for women, or is it something we're being conditioned to demand?

A. It is true that there are a countless number of women like you who never stop to ask themselves if they are missing the Great Experience their friends talk of, figuring, perhaps, that what they've never had they're not going to worry about missing. On the other hand, there are those who, having heard the word orgasm bandied around, begin to resent the fact that something seems to be missing in their marriages.

The mutual delight and satisfaction of *both* partners is desirable. If one ends up dissatisfied, the situation is undesirable, for both, and a frank talk expressing disappointment and equally frank guidance about how to put matters right is needed.

You ask if women are being conditioned to demand total sexual satisfaction. I'm not sure that conditioning is quite the right word. But there *is* a spreading awareness among women that they are not any longer submissive creatures, born to please men, but are equal partners.

Your marriage could be even more satisfactory if you guided your husband to bring you to orgasm. It would bring enrichment to you both.

The sexual revolution has brought about a complete role reversal in some marriages. There are many cases where the wife has to be the main family provider – when the husband, for instance, is disabled or unemployable. She has no other choice. But more and more couples are making a free choice to reverse the husband/wife role. Sometimes the motive is practical: the wife's job, perhaps, is better paid than the husband's. However, in some cases, the husband opts for the role of 'mother' and home-maker while the wife is better equipped to be the provider. For some couples, the arrangement works extremely well, but psychological barriers can hold people back from making the decision to swop.

Q. My wife is a solicitor and has a good and interesting job with much better prospects than mine, which is dull and less well paid. She looks after our home, our two children and does her job perfectly but she constantly complains about the pressures and she gets very tired.

I suggested what I thought was the perfect solution. I would run the home and look after the children. Surprisingly, she opposes the idea. She thinks I will become unmanly and that relatives and neighbours will think the arrangement strange. I do not understand her. She loves her job and is dedicated to women's freedom and my plan would leave her free to develop her talents.

A. I do not think your wife's attitude is difficult to explain, for I imagine she suffers from all the guilts and anxieties common to most career wives. They feel that running the home and taking care of the children somehow helps to expiate the guilt of doing a job they enjoy. The wife who chooses a career feels she must shoulder the burden of doing two jobs. If she lets her family down, she is likely to develop a deep sense of inadequacy as a woman.

I can understand why your wife is fearful that if you took over her home-making role entirely, you'd seem to become less of a man in her eyes. And the opinion of friends and neighbours is, of course, important. She wants you to maintain the head of the house image even though technically you aren't. A lot of liberated women turn out to be less liberated when faced with proving their point. I agree with her that your marriage might be at risk if you carried out your plan.

Perhaps the generation growing up now will not have to face the dilemmas that confront today's citizens in a society where women's role is still changing. The day will surely come when both males and females will take equality for granted. Even very young girls today recognise their right to be equal.

Q. I have read an article you wrote about women being equal and I agree with it. I am eight years old. I went with my brother, who is nine, to join his cub pack but the cub master wouldn't take me when he found out I was a girl. I was very angry.

Don't you think it's wrong for a girl who wants to be a Cub to be made to be a Brownie instead?

Conclusion

'You must,' a man once wrote to me, 'have a very distorted view of marriage, in fact, of life. When I read the letters in your advice column – all of them from people with difficulties and problems – it seems to me that you must have gained the impression that very few people are happy, that marriage as an institution is either sterile or dying or altogether outmoded. You must surely feel that most relationships, whether between husband and wife, lovers, or parents and their children, are discordant. Or do you feel that the number of letters you receive – small, of course, compared to the millions who do not write – represent an unhappy minority? Perhaps there are more contented, well-adjusted people than you may well think.'

This man presented an interesting point of view and it's one shared, I know, by others who believe that the letters I receive must necessarily give me a distorted picture of life.

It is true that perhaps no more than a million or so people a year seek help from advice columnists and other counsellors, although it's impossible to estimate the number in precise terms. Certainly, compared to the total population, the proportion is, indeed, small. But for everyone who seeks help, there must be countless people who struggle on without it or who have no idea where to find it. Nevertheless, I admit to a tendency, at times, to assume that for most, happiness is either fleeting or non-existent, that contentment is a dream out of reach for the majority, that security is something no one can depend on.

After a week of dealing with, perhaps, a thousand or more problem letters, it's hardly surprising that life seems grim and hopeless. Inevitably, I sometimes become despondent. But in less pessimistic moments, I realise that my letters do not necessarily reflect an overall picture of society. Certainly there are happy marriages, contented lovers, devoted parents and loving children. Neighbours are frequently kind and obliging, friends loyal and supportive. Many people are tender towards the elderly and tolerant towards those whose sexual habits and preferences are considered to be outside the norm.

Not everyone has a sexual problem; many husbands are faithful and many wives are caring and considerate. Many people philosophically accept their bumpy noses, their small busts or their bandy legs. Huge numbers of people, in other words, jog along without suffering from a marked neurosis or psychosis. But there cannot be many people who manage to get through their lives without some kind of problem to face. If they're lucky – or clever – if they can count on support from families or friends, if they have someone close with whom they can share their problems, there's no need for them to seek outside help.

There is, indeed, a risk that, as a result of my letters, I could get a soured and jaundiced view of life. But it's encouraging that so many people manage, with or without help, to overcome difficulties and even, in some cases, to gain profit from unhappy experiences.

In the foregoing chapters of this book, the emphasis has been on clearly defined problem areas, many of them sexually based and motivated. To those who say, 'Most of your problems seem to be about sex,' the answer is 'Right'. Most of the problems which beset men and women are, in fact, sexually based. Even the girl who wrote asking me to give her a recipe for yoghurt added that she wanted to impress her boy friend.

There are, of course, a whole range of subjects I deal with that cannot, with the wildest stretch of the imagination, be said to be sexually based: How can I contest a Will? How do I change my name by deed poll? How can I get my money back for a skirt that's fallen to pieces? How can I get a rate rebate, or income tax rebate, or Social Security allowance, or Family Income Supplement, or maintenance or Widow's Pension? Please help – we're threatened with eviction.

Will you write a speech for my husband for our daughter's wedding? Will you suggest a menu for a wedding buffet? Who pays for the flowers and cars? Should I wear long gloves at a cocktail party? What tips should I give when I go on a cruise?

We're coming up to London next week. Will you please suggest a show and restaurant where we can take my mother?

Can you trace my long-lost brother?

Where can I get clothes for extra tall (or short) people? How can I give up smoking/drink/drugs/ fattening foods?

Where can I learn belly-dancing?

How can I get a valuation on my antique clock/auntie's old ornaments/father's old war-medals/a picture I found in the loft?

Sternly, I try to resist the temptation to laugh at some requests but one was entirely irresistible. After a lady read an article about do-it-yourself millinery in a newspaper, she wrote, 'Dear Marje, will you please tell me where I can get felt in Manchester?' I'm ashamed to say I gave in to the temptation to reply, 'You can get felt anywhere, if you put your mind to it.' I added a PS, giving her the name of a department store, hoping she wouldn't walk in saying, 'Where do I get felt here?'

There is a universal assumption that the letters which advice columnists publish are invented – probably by the office boy. When people voice this assumption to me, they still look dubious when I assure them that every published letter is based on a genuine one, rewritten, of course, to conceal the identity of the writer. It would be impossible for anyone to invent the kind of problems I deal with without the actual experience of handling the letters, impossible to know about the anxieties, the frustrations, the dilemmas, the conflicts and the tensions from which so many people suffer.

It is not unusual to cope with more than a thousand problems in a week but it's interesting that the volume of mail has seasonal fluctuations. July, August and December are quiet months. I can only assume that a lot of people are preoccupied with holidays and Christmas shopping, and shelve their worries temporarily. But lonely people write more often during holiday periods, more sharply aware, I conclude, of their feeling of isolation when the rest of the world seems to be enjoying family togetherness.

In September and October, the first results of holiday carelessness become evident. For it's in the early autumn that heartsick girls discover that their early morning sickness is the end product of seaside love. 'I met this Spanish waiter and he said he loved me and he promised he'd come to England and get a job and we'd get married, and he said he'd write every day until we'd meet again and I haven't had a word, not even a postcard. I've written dozens of letters to him and I just can't believe he didn't mean what he said. And now I'm two months overdue and I'm out of my mind with worry. . . .'

Not every holiday romance ends in such dramatic disaster. Some of the sad autumn letters merely describe a broken dream.

January and February are grim months. Pockets are empty. Spirits are low. Problems are magnified and it's the peak period of the year for wives to be abandoned.

My main personal problem in dealing with problem letters is that by the time they reach me, the situation described has all too often reached a stage where little, if anything, can usefully be done to mount a rescue operation. The classic and commonplace letter from the woman who writes, 'After sixteen years of marriage, my husband has walked out, saying he'd found someone more sexually responsive . . .' is typical. If only, I brood, as I try to console her, she'd written when she first began to suspect something was wrong with the marriage. But in many instances, there's a chance, hopefully, to save a situation or dissuade someone from taking a disastrous step.

The girl who thinks that marriage will change her selfish and irresponsible boy friend into a good, dependable husband can be warned that it's highly unlikely. The man who displays unreasonable jealousy before marriage will seldom learn to control it after marriage. The woman who tells me her fiancé, in ungovernable fits of rage, hits her, can be told that his brutality won't stop after the walk down the aisle. A mean man who begrudges every penny during courtship won't suddenly turn into a generous open-handed spouse. The girl who writes about her longing for children by the fiancé who shudders at the thought of them, would be well advised to look for someone who shared her desire for a family; or counselled to sublimate her maternalism in some other way. The woman who asks, 'Will I ever be able to persuade the man I love, who says he'll never marry me, to change his mind?' must be told that it's extremely doubtful.

Big differences in the ages of people contemplating marriage give rise to many doubts. When a man in his fifties writes to say he wonders whether marriage to a girl thirty years his junior could work; or a young man is considering moving in with a woman twice his age, I spell out the dangers. When a white girl asks what chance there is of happiness if she marries her black lover, I tell her of the probable difficulties ahead: the likely prejudice from both blacks and whites, the prejudice their children may face, family resistance and the possible rejection by friends. I stress the need, in such marriages, for absolute certainty that their love for each other is strong enough to overcome the problems they will almost certainly meet.

I always feel that when people, hovering on the brink of a difficult decision, write asking for an opinion about their dilemma, what they're really seeking is an encouraging 'go-ahead' reply from me – a reassurance that everything will work out well in the end. My replies must often be disappointing, for at the back of wavering minds, I suspect there is the hope that doubts will be dispelled by a few comforting words from me.

I should, of course, like to be able to encourage, comfort, reassure and console everyone who writes to me. I should like to think that everyone to whom I have written a letter of advice feels a little better for it or a little more able to face life because of it. But advice columnists aren't oracles, all-wise and all-knowing. A certain amount of expertise, a good deal of experience, involvement and compassion combined with objectivity, are the essential qualifications for the job. Plus a deep interest in the problems and the motivation of those dependent on advice.

Sometimes, at the end of a day of wrestling with people's difficulties and despair, I, too, am despairing: have I been able to help, to comfort, to give new hope when life seems hopeless? This is the time when I need reassurance. But when, at the end of a long, sad letter, a woman writes . . . 'You may not be able to help me, Marje, but I feel so much better for being able to share it all with you,' I feel better, too.